UNIVERSITY of PENNSYLVANIA
PRESS

Since there are and ever were and ever will be variety of opinions, because there is variety of human understandings and uncertainty in things, no man should be too forward in determining all questions nor so forward in prescribing to others, nor invade that liberty which God hath left to us entire. . . .

The Liberty of Prophesying.

THE HOUSE

OF

UNDERSTANDING

Selections from the writings
of JEREMY TAYLOR
by MARGARET GEST

We are all fellow-servants, and not the judge of each other in matters of conscience or doubtful disputation.

The Liberty of Prophesying

PHILADELPHIA
UNIVERSITY OF PENNSYLVANIA PRESS
MCMLIV

Library of Congress Catalog Card Number: 54 — 5011

Published in Great Britain, India, and Pakistan
by Geoffrey Cumberlege: Oxford University Press
London, Bombay, and Karachi

Manufactured in the United States of America

To my father

John Marshall Gest

devoted explorer of old records

ACKNOWLEDGMENTS

My library shelves hold a forbidding set of ten volumes, thick and homely, bound in dull brown calf. On their backs in sturdy gold letters is incised: "Bp. Taylor's Works." A less inviting set of books would be hard to find. Indeed I should never have taken them down were it not that they required the attention of neat's-foot oil. And so I began to explore.

The flyleaves of *The Sermons for the Year* were lined with an engaging variety of citations in my father's neat handwriting, culled from passages in Taylor that obviously had struck his fancy: "The meanest person alive does not think himself fit to be despised"; "Fescennia perfumed her breath not to smell of wine"; "pearls round and orient"; "Can all this rare fabric of heaven and earth come by chance when all the skill of art is not able to make an oyster?" My eye swept down the list, and suddenly I read: "the low-tasted spinage." At once I heard across time and the years, as clearly as could be, my father's voice at the dinner table, "O ho, the low-tasted spinach."

So here is where it came from! Bishop Taylor wrote it three hundred years ago. Well, I said to myself, if Bp. Taylor had such sense, I must certainly look into Bp. Taylor. The result was that I began my present work with the object not of discussing mooted points in Taylor's life and views, but of culling from his vast volumes passages which should represent the man most fully and at his best.

Besides my father, I am greatly indebted to my friend Dr. Miriam M. H. Thrall for assistance in revision of the introduction and arrangement of the excerpts. I take especial pleasure in acknowledging the helpful suggestions of Professor Douglas V. Steere, who most kindly read the manuscript but is in no way responsible for errors. My gratitude is also due to the staffs of the following libraries: Episcopal Divinity School of Philadelphia, Union Theological Seminary of New York, Bryn Mawr College, Haverford College.

MARGARET GEST

Philadelphia
June 1953

CONTENTS

CHRONOLOGICAL TABLE OF THE MORE IMPORTANT DATA

1613 * Jeremy Taylor is baptized in Trinity parish, Cambridge; he was the son of a barber, an occupation which could include pharmacy and surgery.

1626 He enters Caius College, Cambridge University, as a sizar or poor student.

1629 The House of Commons is controlled by Puritans. Parliament is dissolved and does not meet for eleven years.

1633 Taylor receives his M. A. degree and has already been admitted to holy orders. He preaches in St. Paul's and is brought to the attention of Laud, Archbishop of Canterbury.

1635 He receives the M. A. from University College, Oxford.

1636 Laud procures for him a fellowship at All Souls, Oxford; Taylor becomes one of his chaplains.

1638 Taylor becomes rector of Uppingham in Rutlandshire.

1639 Taylor marries Phoebe Langsdale.

1640 Laud is imprisoned. Parliament meets and assumes control.

1642 Civil war breaks out. Taylor is among the first to join the King at Oxford; he serves him as chaplain and may also have been chaplain to the royal army. The bishops are excluded from parliament. A resolution to abolish episcopacy is passed by both houses but is not made effective until 1646. Taylor publishes *Episcopacy Asserted.*

1644 Taylor's parish is sequestered.

1645 He is captured while with the army. Laud is executed. The Puritans suppress the Book of Common Prayer.

1645?-1655? Period of refuge in Wales. During part of this time Taylor is chaplain to the Earl of Carbery at Golden Grove. He reaches the height of his genius as a writer.

1646 He publishes anonymously a defense of the Liturgy, dedicated to "his most sacred Majesty." The King is captured.

1647 In this era of violence and bigotry, *The Liberty of Prophesying* is published; it is generally denounced.

1649 The King is executed. An enlarged edition of Taylor's earlier defense of the Liturgy is published under his own name, with the same dedication. *The Great Exemplar* is published.

* Eden suggests that if the date of his birth were placed a year or two earlier than his baptism, several difficulties in the chronology of his childhood would be removed.

1650 *Holy Living* is published. The Countess of Carbery dies.

1651 Taylor's wife dies. *Holy Dying* is published and also *Sermons for the Summer Half-Year.*

1653 *Sermons for the Winter Half-Year* is published.

1654 Taylor meets John Evelyn.

1655 Taylor publishes *The Golden Grove* and is imprisoned, probably because of its preface. On his release he does not return to Golden Grove.

1655-1658 Period of severe persecution and poverty. Taylor is for some time in seclusion in Wales. In 1655 *Unum Necessarium* is published, bringing upon him a storm of disapproval. Probably by 1655 he is married to Mrs. Joanna Bridges, who survives him. He officiates in private congregations, sometimes in or near London, and in this capacity is often in considerable danger. Evelyn and others shield him. He is again imprisoned.

1658-1667 Period in Ireland.

1658 Taylor accepts a joint lectureship at Lisburn, in northeast Ireland, a locality filled with hostile Presbyterians. He lives on the estate of his patron, the Earl of Conway, and becomes chaplain. Cromwell dies and the Presbyterians thereafter assert themselves even more vigorously.

1659 Taylor loses his lectureship. He is arrested twice at the instigation of the Presbyterians.

1660 The monarchy is restored. Taylor publishes *The Worthy Communicant;* also *Ductor Dubitantium,* on which he has been working for approximately twenty years. He is appointed vice-chancellor of the University of Dublin.

1661 He is consecrated bishop of Down and Connor and is given oversight of the small diocese of Dromore. He becomes a member of the Irish Privy Council. As bishop he is opposed by the Presbyterian ministers, who refuse to recognize his authority or conform to Anglican service. He dismisses thirty-six of them. He preaches his sermon before the Irish parliament, in which he states his case in regard to those who rebel against authority.

1662 He preaches his great sermon to the University of Dublin.

1664 The first part of *Dissuasive from Popery* is published.

1667 Taylor dies at Lisburn and is buried in the cathedral at Dromore. The second part of the *Dissuasive* is published posthumously.

God enkindles charity upon a variety of means and instruments, by a thought, by a chance, by a text of scripture, by a natural tenderness, by the sight of a dying or a tormented beast.

The Great Exemplar

•

We can no more be removed from the presence of God than from our own being . . . . God is everywhere present by His power. He rolls the orbs of heaven with His hand; He fixes the earth with His foot; He guides all the creatures with His eye, and refreshes them with His influence . . . . In the wilderness, the bittern and the stork, the dragon and the satyr, the unicorn and the elk, live upon His provisions and revere His power, and feel the force of His almightiness.

Holy Living

[Men's] pleasure dies like the time in which it danced awhile; and when the minute is gone, so is the pleasure too, and leaves no footstep but the impression of a sigh, and dwells nowhere but in the same house where you shall find yesterday.

Sermon XX for the Summer Half-Year

JEREMY TAYLOR

In Jeremy Taylor's six thousand pages there is an ancient wisdom interwoven with a liberal and modern tolerance; he is spiritual, witty, and learned, curious in his turns and sudden changes of thought. Since many of his best passages, however, are buried in a theological matrix now for the most part long outdated, we need access in convenient form to the various phases of his extraordinary mind.

Yet collections of excerpts from Taylor's writings have been all too few and not, in a comprehensive sense, representative. Grateful as we are for the compilation of Logan Pearsall Smith, we need a more inclusive view of Taylor if we are to recover in his work the whole man: deeply religious and human, a leader who had the initiative and insight to think his way to essentials, and the perseverance to uphold them through years of confusion and danger.

By a trick of fate Taylor in popular opinion has become classed as a stylist and to a strange extent denied the role of thinker. The exuberant encomiums of Coleridge, who rediscovered Taylor for the nineteenth century and placed him beside Shakespeare, Bacon and Milton, were chorused by the other leading Romantic critics—Lamb, Hazlitt, and De Quincey. Yet in this chorus there was an occasional note of discord. Coleridge's idolatry of Taylor fell only short of his idolatry of Shakespeare, but during his extravagant eulogy he referred to the great seventeenth-century divine as "all weatherbeaten, dim, useless, a *Ghost* in *marble.*" [1] Too often this highly quotable censure has been accepted as unquestionably as the ardent praise, and Coleridge's estimate has from time to time recurred through the intervening years essentially unchanged.

Both Sir Edmund Gosse, Taylor's distinguished Victorian biographer, and Logan Pearsall Smith have carried on the disparagement as well as the extravagant eulogy. To the substance of Taylor's work Smith gives scant attention, remarking that "his most fervent admirers have to admit that his mental powers were somewhat limited and commonplace, and that he failed in handling the larger questions of religious thought," and " 'had no ideas.' " [2] It is the enchantment of Taylor's style, the vivacity and music of his imagery, that holds this last of the great purists spellbound.

"We still read, or still should read," Smith tells us,[3] "his tremulous pages for the beauty of the world which hung upon his pen, a world full of sun and the shimmer of water, a world delicately tinted, fleeting, evanescent, and yet fixed and made imperishable by the incantation of his words." Smith speaks of Taylor's "minute, almost microscopic observation" and of his "revelation in the music and magic of words of a unique vision." In detailed analysis he shows us how Taylor was "a master of that verbal music, that felicity of sound and rhythm, which is the basis, the fundamental quality, of this audible art of language." "Now and then," he comments, "as we read him an imagination, radiant and strange, seems to unfold its wings and soar aloft; now and then this painful clergyman, as he writes down his arguments and expositions, seems to dip his pen in enchanted ink; the words begin to dance and glitter, and a splendour falls upon the illuminated page. And when this happens the effect is so surprising that it seems the result of a spell, an incantation, a kind of magic."

These delightfully phrased comments are sensitive and discriminating. Yet it is not Taylor as stylist but as man of thought for whom we have most need. He is often inconsistent and redundant, often conspicuously uneven; he formulated no system of theology or philosophy, nor did he attempt to synthesize the ideas of others. For all that, he was a great thinker, brilliant in his expositions of tolerance, in his psychological insight, and in his keen understanding of the good and evil forces in society. As a prophet, in a period of civil war and bigotry, he urged search for truth, for sane living, for tolerance, for God.

It is strange that Gosse, who admired Taylor's great book on tolerance, *A Discourse of the Liberty of Prophesying,* should have fallen into the Coleridgian error of finding the famous bishop deficient in the field of thought. Tullock had previously emphasized the importance of this book pleading for tolerance, for freedom of belief and worship; and Gosse himself, praising the originality of Taylor's point of view and his "intellectual and moral liberality," had enthusiastically written: "There is, perhaps, no man to-day in England, who worships, or who worships not, as his conscience bids him, who does not owe a fraction of his peace to Jeremy Taylor." [4]

Had Taylor written nothing but this courageous and enlightened plea for tolerance and liberty of conscience, we should have in this book alone ample basis for refutation of Coleridge's quotable stricture. Today there is far less faith in systems of thought and the efficacy of academic logic than there was when Coleridge wrote in the early nineteenth century, or even than there was when Smith wrote in 1930. We need as urgently as did the seventeenth century a prophet of peace and moderation with the courage to preach tolerance, the brotherhood of man, the fatherhood of God.

That Taylor produced no system of philosophy is not surprising. The Bible together with the tenets and service of the Anglican Church satisfied his own needs too fully for him to turn to philosophical speculation for evidence of the existence of God and man's relation to Him. An ardent divine, he was deeply religious himself and constantly concerned with his duties as a preacher and confessor in a period of martyrdom, when men sorely needed personal guidance and spiritual support.

It is this attitude that gives to Taylor's writing at its best a spirituality, sanity, and an unusual awareness of mental states. Not only is his observation acute; the conclusions which he draws are at times startlingly modern, as for example the comment: "Some men are affrighted from their cradle in some instances . . . and the fears of childhood are not shaken from the conscience in old age." In expressing his delight in children and his understanding of their moods, Taylor is almost unique in his own day, anticipating nineteenth-century interest. Taylor's greatness, indeed, far from being limited to his style, lies in his amazing erudition, his spirituality, his psychological approach, and his prophetic defense of man's psychological and religious need to follow the dictates of his own conscience. His spirit, to take one of his own metaphors from its context, dwelt in a "house of understanding."

It is only fair to state that Taylor's contemporaries were as much impressed by the beauty and variety of his style as have been his recent admirers and critics. And the style is indeed astonishing. In his most characteristic work his control of pace does not falter, the shifts in speed and rhythm being made neatly and with no more apparent effort than those of a thoroughbred horse. He has at times the beauty of biblical cadence; at times he approaches a modern staccato effect befitting some blunt or whimsical turn of thought; at moments of passion he can command a torrential cacophony which is almost overwhelming.

The encyclopedic range, if not the accuracy, of Taylor's learning has also never been questioned. His knowledge of the early Christian Fathers, begun in his student days at Cambridge, is intimate and wide. Equally comprehensive is his reading in Greek and Latin historians and in medieval scholars. In his pages appear classical poets, dramatists, orators, philosophers, Hebrew prophets and rabbis. There are Arabic legends and French romances. Scattered through his volumes are over 680 references to Augustine, 125 to Origen, 70 to Euripides, 135 to Horace, 75 to Ovid, and 250 to Plutarch, to name a few of the multitude of authors he mentions.

Taylor's acquisitive mind was also stocked with a curious assortment of information from books and the world around him. Like his friend Evelyn, the horticulturist, he was a close observer of nature, even noting the social habits of plants, a science that gardeners are only now beginning to study. Bishop Heber, his authoritative biographer, describes Taylor's *Ductor Dubitantium* as an ancient, inlaid cabinet, "whose multifarious contents perplex our choice, and offer to the admiration or curiosity of a more accurate age a vast wilderness of trifles and varieties . . . whose ebony drawers and perfumed recesses contain specimens of every thing that is precious or uncommon, and many things for which a modern museum might be searched in vain."[5]

Even when this wealth of information becomes almost unbearably didactic and tedious, Taylor usually escapes being the pedant. Coleridge in renewed and heightened adulation records: "But take him all in all, such a miraculous combination of erudition . . . of logic subtle as well as acute, and as robust as agile; of psychological insight, so fine yet so secure! . . . I believe such a complete man hardly shall we meet again."[6]

From the moment Taylor first risked his life in the cause of his king, Charles I, he lived boldly, speaking his mind fearlessly as his conscience dictated. As early as 1642, two years after his patron, Archbishop Laud, had been imprisoned, and only a short time before the livings of Anglican clergy were sequestered, Taylor in the face of persecution wrote his *Episcopacy Asserted.* It is a reactionary work; he bases his argument on doubtful assumptions and obscures his ground by lengthy didacticisms. Indeed, the only thing to his credit is that he had the hardihood to write the book at all—which is credit enough, considering the times.

Quite as courageous as his defense of the Church was his attempt to liberalize it. In opposition to his superiors he championed the principle of liberty of conscience and denounced the orthodox doctrine of predestination, which deprived man of freedom of choice. In particular he found the implication that unbaptized infants were objects of God's wrath to be offensive to reason and the heart. These views indeed were so boldly expressed that it is to the credit and glory of the Anglican Church that it did not dismiss him. However heated the disputes within that Church became, it remained vast and inclusive, capable of housing the saintly George Herbert and others of the metaphysical poets, the eloquent and learned Bishop Andrewes, the High-Churchman Laud, Henry More the transcendentalist, Donne the poet and preacher, and the apostles of freedom of conscience, Hales, Chillingworth, and Taylor himself.

* * *

Before reading Jeremy Taylor it is well to recall that the seventeenth century in England was an age, like our own, of upheaval, of new forces contending with old. On the one hand there was a search and passion for truth and freedom; on the other a loyalty to tradition and a reverence for authority. In politics, the Parliamentarians rebelled against a despotic government and the Divine Right of Kings, but found support for their own rights in the rediscovered Anglo-Saxon laws, and beheaded their monarch. In the conflict between authority and freedom, Bacon upset the old laws of philosophy and led the revolt in which medieval scholastic theory gave way to observation of fact. The microscope showed new and startling worlds in man and nature. The telescope put man in his place in the universe and brought about a mental revolution of almost incalculable importance. Pepys, with such an instrument on top of his house, could see for himself the newly discovered worlds, even while in his immemorial diary he was painstakingly delineating the minutiae and ephemera of social life. With characteristic vigor John Donne started the revolt against the old unrealistic conventions of poetry, and Milton vehemently pleaded for freedom in religion, politics, and the press. The search for truth led to one of the first biblical criticisms, Hobbes's contention that the Pentateuch was not written by Moses.

There was collecting and classifying and evaluating the past as well as investigating fresh fields of science. While John Evelyn, the horticulturist and diarist, was writing about fruit trees, the education of children, and architecture, Robert Cotton was collecting practically everything of antiquity he could lay hands on; he had a passion for marbles, manuscripts, oddities, and his great library was generously available to scholars. Dugdale was doing his history of Warwickshire and making drafts of the monuments in ancient monasteries. Selden, the jurist and oriental scholar, was writing, among other things, the history of English law down to Henry II, a treatise on marriage and divorce among the Jews, and his great *Titles of Honour,* still the most trustworthy work of its kind. There is a liveliness and vivacity in much of the writing of the time, even on the most unlikely subjects: Father Paul Sarpi's *Council of Trent,* though in translation, has an ease, an unstraining wit, and a pace that carries one with it, as has that engaging volume by John Weever, *Funeral Monuments.*

In 1613, in the city of Cambridge, Jeremy Taylor was baptized. He had the eagerness, vigor, and intensity of his age, its salty wit and its passion for reason. Like the better-known men of letters with the exception of Milton and Marvel, Taylor supported the King in the civil war with the Roundheads. By 1633 he had been admitted to holy orders in the Church of England, and when the royal army was centered at Oxford, he at once joined the King as chaplain, and was captured and imprisoned in 1645. After the Roundheads gained the upper hand and persecution of his Church became general, he was deprived of his parish but found a protector and patron in Richard Vaughan, Earl of Carbery, at whose mansion in Wales, Golden Grove, much of his most brilliant work was written. Fortunately he later found another friend and patron in John Evelyn, fortunately, because Evelyn had influence with both of the chief factions in England. It was in part through Evelyn that Taylor at one time was released from prison, and eventually, to ensure his safety, was offered a lectureship at Lisburn, Ireland; here Taylor went in 1658 under the protection of Cromwell, who was undoubtedly glad to get such antagonistic eloquence out of England.

At the Restoration, instead of being recalled to England, as he had hoped, Taylor was appointed to the see of Down and Connor, and made vice-chancellor of the University of Dublin. Yet in spite of these honors his life in Ireland was far from pleasant. He was surrounded by a refractory clergy and a rebellious people; he was isolated from his friends in England, and missed intercourse with lively and well-informed minds.

We sense in Taylor a warmly affectionate man. He loved his God, his Church, and his King, and people and nature and the very process of living. In the two periods of his life when he had means, his generous temperament and his fondness for music led to his building at his own expense an organ for his church at Uppingham and later, in Ireland, to his rebuilding the choir of the cathedral at Dromore. Taylor is reported to have had a remarkably beautiful speaking voice and also to have been blessed with good looks. It is an indication of his charm as well as of his talents that he had the gift of attracting friends—a fortunate gift, as he was often to be poor and often in danger.

Early in Taylor's life Archbishop Laud discovered his ability, appointed him one of his chaplains, and procured for him a fellowship at All Souls, Oxford, a center of active and liberal theology. This association with liberal thinkers is significant because Taylor during his years as an undergraduate at Cambridge had been subjected to the medieval system of studies still prevailing at the Universities, which the less conformative scholar, Milton, stigmatized as "that asinine feast of sowthistles and brambles." Since Taylor had gained at Cambridge a fondness for the lore of the Schoolmen and early Christian Fathers, he was fortunate in also acquiring the antidote of forward trends.

From the beginning, it is evident that Taylor liked the amenities of good food and good conversation and good manners. He stressed and practised courtesy to servants in an age when that graciousness was evidently rare. In Ireland, on an occasion when a servant declared he had seen a ghost, Taylor interviewed the friends of the dead man. "It was pleasant," writes Taylor's secretary, "to hear my lord talk with these poor people . . . on the subject of their relation's spectre."

A sense for law and order and a deep reverence for authority were, on the one hand, among Taylor's cardinal traits; on the other, was his bold advocacy of liberty in matters pertaining to conscience. Between the two he was often torn, yet he never forgot that religion *is* goodness and that intercourse with God can alone produce it and guide man in moments of conflicting loyalties.

Jeremy Taylor was married twice; in each case apparently happily. "Nothing," he says, "can sweeten felicity itself, but love."

He died in 1667 at Lisburn.

* * *

In Taylor's stout volumes, one strain runs through all the varied pages, whether he is writing in a magnificent rush of words or in the tediousness of his casuistry, and this is his love of God. Christocentric he certainly was in his theology, and he loved very deeply his Lord Jesus, but God was his center and God was the force that drove him onward through all his difficult years.

At first reading, Taylor's idea of the worship of God may seem like that of any other highly religious person. However, we find, scattered through his volumes, passages which show he was familiar with that phase of worship known as contemplation, or mysticism (to use this word of many connotations in its narrowest sense): harmony, or fusion, with transcendent reality, a state in which barriers between the individual and God are overcome. This exalted union, the contemplatives tell us, carries a realization of certainty, illumination, ineffability. Such is the consensus of opinion of those who have experienced contemplation, regardless of country or creed or century. Progression in this worship usually conforms to an organic growth, a life pattern, there being, as Taylor describes in *The Great Exemplar,* stages through which the novice must pass, all entailing the most concentrated dedication.

In Taylor's publications there is nothing, as far as the present writer can see, to prove that he himself attempted to practice contemplation, although his sermon to the students of Dublin University describes this state of religious ecstasy with a personalized detail which may indicate his own experience. But a letter to Evelyn, dated 1659, from Ireland, leaves no doubt that he sought fulfillment in this exalted state of worship.

"I promise to myselfe," writes Taylor, "that I may receive from you an excellent account of your progression in religion, and that you are entered into the experimental and secret way of it, which is that state of excellency whether [whither] good persons use to arrive after a state of repentance and caution. My retirement in this solitary place hath been, I hope, of some advantage to me as to this state of religion, in which I am yet but a novice, but by the goodness of God I see fine things before me whither I am contending. It is a great but a good worke, and I beg of you to assist me with your prayers, and to obtaine of God for me that I may arrive to that height of love and union with God, which is given to all those soules who are very deare to God."[7]

Perhaps Taylor finally attained to "that height of love" where such "fine things" awaited him. It is not unlikely, for he has one of the hallmarks of contemplatives, common even to the most learned and eloquent of them: the realization that there are no words to express this highest state of worship, for the brain cannot report divine knowledge. In his sermon to the young men of Dublin University, he says that the secret can only be *felt:* the man who is holy "feels this unintelligible mystery, and sees with his heart what his tongue can never express and his metaphysics can never prove."

* * *

In an age of religious strife, it is interesting to note that Taylor had the strength uniformly to denounce controversies, even when he himself was drawn into them. Throughout his life he remained consistently tolerant as far as questions of dogma were concerned. From his own experience he saw how difficult it is to arrive at steadfast conclusions. "I find," he writes with humility, "that the more I search, the further I am from being satisfied, and make but few discoveries save of my own ignorance." And again: "Indeed it is a very hard thing for a man to know his own heart."

In his personal relationships, also, Taylor was tolerant, for he became a friend of Christopher Davenport, a Franciscan. This friendship, together with his love of ritual and his connection with the High-Churchman Laud, was a cause of the suspicion that Taylor was attracted to Roman Catholicism, a suspicion that was destined to haunt him all his life, although he devotedly proclaimed that the Church of England was "the best Church in the world," and his *Dissuasive from Popery* eventually discredited the charge.

Yet perhaps it is not strange that Taylor often puzzled his contemporaries. A man who seeks moderation, the mediative course, may easily appear inconsistent. Furthermore, although Taylor was liberal where questions of dogma were concerned, he was rigid in his insistence that the ritual of his Church should be observed. His feeling would seem to have been somewhat like that of the wise Greeks in the Eleusinian mysteries who discovered that a ritual is desirable as a binding force, and yet they left the worshiper free where freedom is important, in the sphere of thought. The Greeks, in the words of Jane E. Harrison, conformed in the outward acts, but knew that in every sacrament was to be found "the only thing you could find—what you brought."[8]

Taylor felt that every man had the right to decide what tenets he should accept. Dogma should not be prescribed; there should be liberty of conscience. For himself, belief in God was derived from the Bible and from the Anglican articles of faith. But in addition to these, he recognized that it was also derived from the worshiper's own perception: "I believe a God," he says in astounding detail, "because the sun is a glorious body; or because of the variety of plants, or the fabric and rare contexture of a man's eye."

Taylor's bold championing of liberty of conscience, men's right to believe as they wished, places him among the vanguard of his age. In order to understand the significance of his great book, *The Liberty of Prophesying,* or the right to profess one's own interpretation of the Scriptures, it is necessary to keep in mind the political, philosophical, and theological contentions and confusions of his day. Although scholasticism still held sway in the universities, elsewhere the developments of science and the new philosophy of reason were rapidly gaining ground in spite of opposition. The materialist Hobbes, in line with the trend of science, maintained that there was no proof of anything beyond what is apprehended by the senses, and thus repudiated the spiritual side of man's nature. His forceful book, *The Leviathan,* speeded the growth of materialism, since it put in new dress the reactionary idea that to attain peace all the rights of the people must be merged in the State, or Leviathan, all citizens' responsibility subservient to a central authority. To the disillusioned, sick of theological and political revolutions, such a simple solution was a relief, but to many others the renunciation of the people's rights was terrifying, and the denial of the spirit a source of deep concern.

In France, Descartes reasserted the world of the spirit as well as that of matter, yet each of these spheres was for him distinctive; neither could enter the other. It was to bridge that gap and to combat ecclesiastical dogmatism as well as Hobbism that the Cambridge Platonists arose. These mystical philosophers were repelled by what they considered harsh Puritan doctrine as much as they were by High-Church ritualism, yet they were themselves religious and labored to fuse philosophy with religion in the light of the new scientific learning with its emphasis on reason and free inquiry. The human intellect, they maintained, is "the candle of the Lord." In fact, the Platonists, among them Cudworth, Henry More, and John Smith, constituted the only group in England that could meet with a well-ordered philosophy the challenge of materialism. Hobbes, they stated, was wrong in exploiting science with the effect of negating religion; and in opposition they contended that science and the new philosophy of reason instead of fostering heresy and atheism could actually increase man's knowledge of God. To Henry More there was a continuity in nature and man, and man and God; he found the cleavage of spirit and matter not in accord with his reason and experience, and quoting Neoplatonic writers he argued that the highest truth can be grasped only through something in us of the divine. Cudworth maintained that man is divine if there is any divinity at all, and Smith felt that to gain true knowledge we must "open that brighter eye of our understanding, the other eye of the soul."

Taylor, in spite of his predilection for the ancients, was by no means unappreciative of his contemporaries and immediate predecessors. For "the great Erasmus" and "the incomparable Mr. Hooker" he had the highest regard. Hobbes he alludes to once, somewhat disparagingly, although he termed him "a late witty man"; and Galileo and Descartes he called the "excellent persons of yesterday." He was deeply read in Episcopius and Grotius. His writings on tolerance develop the thought of John Hales and more especially William Chillingworth, and there is some evidence that he may, consciously or unconsciously, have borrowed insignificantly from the sermons of Hales and the Cambridge Platonist, John Smith. Resemblance to the sermons of Donne would seem to spring from the fact that both men were poetical and that Donne earlier had helped to give all seventeenth-century prose as well as poetry its basic imagery, sentence flow, and idiom.

Certainly Taylor was acquainted with the Platonists and they with him, though whether either directly influenced the other on metaphysical questions would be difficult to prove, since the Cambridge scholars reached their conclusions chiefly through philosophical disquisition, and Taylor's approach was theological, often personal. Mysticism, which was strong on the Continent, was in the English air, to be traced in some of the prose and more of the so-called metaphysical poetry. It is most frequent in George Herbert, Vaughan, Donne, Traherne, Crashaw, while from across the English Channel came perhaps, along with much else, Pascal's final testimony to mystical experience. Throughout the century, mysticism may be said to have held its own against the growing influence of materialistic ideologies.

An exponent of mystical thought whom Taylor avowedly failed to appreciate was George Fox, the founder of the small sect of Quakers, who felt that an "inner light" revealed the presence of God in man. Fox taught the validity of conscience as opposed to creeds, and direct revelation from God by way of contemplation as opposed to ritual and dogma. His denunciation of all ritual, however, aroused dislike and suspicion in many of even the most liberal minds. It is not surprising that Taylor, with his reverence for the rites of his Church and his insistence on their importance, could not understand this sect, although its contemplative core was very like his own. The Quakers were thought to disregard authority; the liberal Evelyn writes in his diary that they "shew no respect to any man, magistrate or not." Taylor, with his respect for established government and its officers, and his reverence for "the person of the prince," would naturally be distrustful of them on this score also.

Yet the Quakers, with the Cambridge philosophers and Taylor himself in his *Liberty of Prophesying,* exerted their force, however slight, to combat the more narrow phases of Protestantism which in the heat of the day were often a menace to spiritual freedom.

It will be recalled that soon after its establishment, the Church of England had been split by the Puritans, as the Low-Churchmen were originally called, who thought the High Church was inclined to Rome. They set up their own form of church government and brought from abroad a Calvinian Presbyterianism, an importation that resulted in fierce ideological struggles.

Some of the thorniest of these concerned original sin, free will, and predestination, in varying shades of modification. The extremists maintained that salvation depended solely on an almighty decree, for the corrupt nature of man (inherited, it was held, from his ancestor Adam) prevented him from contributing anything toward his own salvation. If he had been predestined to be damned, no matter how hard he worked, he would be impotent to save himself. This implied an irrevocable partition of the human race into the saved and the not-saved.

The doctrine in its strictest aspects had been promulgated by St. Augustine, and although it had been eloquently combatted by the great heretic Pelagius, it had entered in varying degrees into Christian dogma: it was included in the decrees of the Council of Trent and, also in its extreme form, in the Lambeth Articles of the Church of England in the time of Queen Elizabeth I. Although those articles never received official sanction, they were accepted by the more orthodox Churchmen. The doctrine had, however, never been applied in its full force until it became an important tenet of the Calvinists.

It was a theory against which liberal thinkers had rebelled and were to continue to rebel, for they felt that the justice of God is certainly as much of His essence as is His power. The leader of a distinguished group of anti-Calvinists was Arminius, that rare Dutch preacher who at the beginning of the seventeenth century emphasized man's own will, as well as God's, as a determinant of salvation.

Needless to say, the Arminians' anti-Calvinism met with violent opposition; politics entered, and on all sides angry disputes arose over free will, predestination, and redemption. On the one hand, liberal trends were deepened in the Church; on the other, rancor and suspicion of heresy were aroused in the minds of the orthodox.

The followers of Arminius, headed by the equally important Episcopius, became more than merely another new sect. Realizing that they must prove their contentions by biblical arguments, they studied the Bible afresh, interpreting it according to its "native and literal sense" as they would any other book, and so opened the way to modern historical criticism. The Arminians saw and opposed the evil in creeds and formularies; they noted that dogmas tended to become so much the Word of God that anyone who deviated from them by an iota was considered a heretic. Even daring to question the value of dogma altogether, they based their Christianity on the Bible and the Apostles' Creed, and swung back to the precepts and simplicity of the primitive Church. As a result, conciliatory tolerance and liberty of free inquiry were reasserted in Protestanism; the liberal atmosphere thus created was highly sympathetic to men of thoughtful minds, among them Taylor.

In 1647 when about thirty-four Taylor published his *Liberty of Prophesying*, that stirring plea, already referred to, for freedom of the individual's conscience, and for the right of every man to interpret the Scriptures. He was among the first to grasp the truth, and perhaps the first to state it fully, that religion and politics are not inseparably allied; "the ecclesiastical power," he says, "is not of capacity to use the temporal sword. . . . Doctrines and opinions of men are things spiritual, and therefore not cognoscible by a temporal authority."

Taylor's stand appears the more courageous when one remembers the conditions under which he wrote. In the England of 1647, religious belief was conceived to be not an opinion but a law. Persecution was regarded as a legitimate means of enforcing uniformity, and obstinate "heretics" expressing opinions at variance with the prevailing power could be handed over to the civil authorities for torture and imprisonment and sometimes death. The right of an individual to interpret Scripture was not to be tolerated. Taylor's great work was the first that fully and comprehensively brought liberty of opinion, as we know it today, to the attention of the English conscience. The book was novel when it appeared, and after three hundred years it is not outdated.

In an age of hair-splittings and angry theological disputes, Taylor opposed the almost universal conviction that belligerent loyalty to sects is a virtue. He insisted that there could be unity in essentials and at the same time an amiable tolerance for a diversity of details.

Mischiefs, he says, proceed not from the fact that all men are not of one mind, for that is neither necessary nor possible; the trouble is that "every opinion is made an article of faith, every article is a ground of a quarrel, every quarrel makes a faction, every faction is zealous, and all zeal pretends for God. . . . We think we love not God except we hate our brother, and we have not the virtue of religion unless we persecute all religions but our own."

By his courageous defense of freedom of conscience, the liberty of all men to express themselves according to their own sense of right, and the obligation of all men to grant such liberty to others, Taylor places himself among the world's great apostles of freedom and tolerance, several of whom had come shortly before his own time. From the opening of the sixteenth century there had been a desire to look again at the Scriptures in the light of reason and free inquiry. Erasmus had maintained that one could remain within the Church, in his day the Roman Catholic Church, and accept a few simple bases of belief, yet hammer at abuses. At the Council of Trent, just a hundred years before Taylor's *Liberty,* John Baptista Cigala, the Romanist bishop of Albenga, interrupted the discussions of doctrines and heresies with a vehement and common-sense defense of tolerance. It was never, he asserted,[9] found in any story that a man was willing to have his idea condemned; if his opinion was rejected he would defend it more obstinately. It is by these means that heresies spring. The best thing to do is to tolerate all opinions, for without this moderation every little verbal difference is able to divide the world.

Coming nearer to his own day, Taylor's "incomparable Mr. Hooker" held that the Church could be tolerantly comprehensive of all Christian activities. In Holland, Grotius, theologian and international lawyer, who was attracted to Roman Catholicism as well as to Arminianism, thought it reasonable for men to waive their differences for the sake of peace, and keep silent on their own opinions. He was much read and admired by Taylor, his views, particularly in the matter of original sin, probably having a good deal to do with Taylor's own.

Other important influences on Taylor were, as we have said, John Hales and William Chillingworth. After attending the synod of Dort in 1618, from which in the midst of polemic violence and ill feeling the Arminian representatives were dismissed, and indeed banished from Holland, Hales insisted that theological and dogmatic differences are not religious differences, and should not break the unity of faith and worship. In 1637 Chillingworth wrote that the matters which separate sects of Christians are not matters of faith but matters of speculation on which they may differ safely. Every man is to judge and interpret Scripture for himself. The Apostles' Creed he would have the basis of reunion; there must not be zealous Papists, Calvinists, or Lutherans, but plain and honest Christians. Chillingworth catches fire at the thought of religious liberty. "Take away these walls of separation, and all will quickly be one. Take away this persecuting, burning, cursing, damning of men for not subscribing to the words of men as the words of God . . . . In a word, take away tyranny." [10]

In the ten years between the publication of Chillingworth's book and Taylor's *Liberty,* the government and the Church of England had been overthrown, the King captured, the highhanded Laud beheaded. The Presbyterians had triumphed, and they in turn had been defeated by the Independents, who were somewhat more tolerant. Strange sects were multiplying on all sides: Anti-Scripturists, Familists, and a score of others. In the midst of this confusion and discord, Taylor brought forward his new plan for amity.

In the *Liberty,* Taylor like Chillingworth cuts swiftly and sharply through the accepted premise that sectarian beliefs are fundamentals of Christianity. Rather, he says, the Church must rest on a broad basis of goodness and piety; repeatedly he insists that "a holy life will make our belief holy." He held that since sects, though important, are not of the essence, they should not be the grounds of quarrels and of exclusion. As to the actual form of church government, although he believed episcopacy to be "the best Church in the world," his convictions on this point did not prevent him from feeling that there should be complete tolerance in these matters among all sects of the Christian Church. From Anabaptists to Papists, all who followed Christ, all who professed the shortest and oldest creed, the Apostles' Creed, he would acknowledge as fellow-members, even though they held varying opinions in lesser matters. Without qualification he states:

"We are all fellow-servants, and not the judge of each other in matters of conscience or doubtful disputation. . . . It is a hard case that we should think all Papists, and Anabaptists, and Sacramentaries, to be fools and wicked persons; certainly among all these sects there are very many wise men and good men. . . . Why then should I hate such persons whom God loves and who love God . . . [who] have not the same opinions I have, and do not determine their school-questions to the sense of my sect?"

Here Taylor is far and away beyond Grotius, whose advice is to concede and "keep silent" unless in a position of authority, or Chillingworth, who proposes that in the Christian church there should be no sects but "all plain and honest Christians." For Taylor sees farther, in that he advocates different sects within the general Church and a "liberty of disagreeing." He has the shrewd belief that peace may be more nearly attained if differences are not repressed but freely discussed and aired. Moreover, such discussion might lead, he affirms, not only to greater knowledge but to greater unity and more brilliant vision.

> "Although the Spirit of God did rest upon us in divided tongues, yet so long as those tongues were of fire not to kindle strife but to warm our affections and inflame our charities, we should find that this variety of opinions in several persons would be looked upon as an argument only of diversity of operations, while the Spirit is the same. . . . And if we all impartially endeavour to find a truth, since this endeavour and search only is in our power . . . I can see no reason why this pious endeavour to find out truth shall not be of more force to unite us in the bonds of charity than the misery in missing it shall be to disunite us. . . .
>
> For if it be evinced that one heaven shall hold men of several opinions, if the unity of faith be not destroyed by that which men call differing religions, and if an unity of charity be the duty of us all, even towards persons that are not persuaded of every proposition we believe, then I would fain know to what purpose are all those stirs and great noises in Christendom."

To Taylor the Bible was religion: all articles of faith are set down in the Bible, but it was difficult to know how to interpret Scripture. He insists that each man's painstaking search of the Bible in the light of his reason must be the final authority as to its truth for him. Except for the Bible, all sources of authority can err: ecclesiastical councils, the Pope, the Fathers, all dogmas. Only rituals are to be considered authoritative, the most ancient symbols of divinity that we have. "There is scarce anything . . . that can with any confidence of argument pretend to derive from the apostles, except rituals and manners of ministration." In his exception of rituals he foreshadows the theory which Frazer made the cornerstone of his great work, *The Golden Bough,* the fact that ritual remains constant while myth changes. "No doctrines," says Taylor, "or speculative mysteries are so transmitted to us by so clear a current that we may see a visible channel and trace it to the primitive fountains."

It is significant that, in an age when deviation by a hairsbreadth from dogma constituted heresy, Taylor should have denied its authority. For him a good life justified the creed held; if beliefs were honestly arrived at no man should be judged a heretic.

Tolerance and charity run through his great book: "Faith is not only a precept of doctrines but of manners and holy life." His fellowship would extend to all: "What is it to me if the Greek Church denies procession of the third Person from the second, so she will give me the right hand of friendship though I affirm it?"

In fact Taylor's plea for the hated sect of Anabaptists was so fair, and gave so much emphasis to their admirable traits, that he was later obliged to add an appendix to the *Liberty* to show that he had not meant to weaken the "right side." Like Erasmus, he felt that all sides of any point of contention should be represented.

This insistence on the right to speak the truth as it appears at any individual moment opened Taylor, as it had Grotius, to the charges of inconsistency, ambiguity, and vacillation; we like our theologians to stick to one definite view, to have unwavering opinions; and even ardent admirers, as we have found, are aware of Taylor's lapses of logic, his swinging from one side of a question to the other. For Taylor boldly and constantly asserted what seemed to him justice, even if it involved contradictions. As he was to say in his *Deus Justificatus,* "I must go after truth wherever it is." Thus he finds that tolerance and liberty when applied to the conduct of public affairs can slip into license and anarchy. He is very firm in asserting the need of law and order and established government, a point to remember when considering his future actions in Ireland, where his severity with the rebellious Presbyterian clergy was harshly criticized as inconsistent with his views expressed in the *Liberty.* Whatsoever, he said, is "destructive to human society and the public and just interests of bodies politic is out of the limits of my question, and does not pretend to compliance or toleration: so that I allow no indifferency nor any countenance to those religions whose principles destroy government."

Taylor ended the second edition of the *Liberty* with the following charming story from the Persian poet, Saadi:

Abraham, sitting at his tent door, espied an old man, weary with travel and his hundred years of age. Abraham washed his feet and gave him supper. But when the old man admitted that he worshiped only the fire, not the God of Heaven, Abraham thrust him out into the perils of the night. God asked Abraham where the stranger was, and Abraham replied, "I thrust him away because he did not worship Thee." Then God admonished, "I have suffered him these hundred years, although he dishonoured Me, and couldst thou not endure him one night when he gave thee no trouble?" Upon this, Abraham fetched the old man back and gave him hospitable entertainment.

"Go thou and do likewise," Taylor tells his readers, "and thy charity will be rewarded by the God of Abraham."

Needless to say, at the time of its publication the *Liberty's* idea of freedom of opinion was, with a few exceptions, condemned as heretical by Anglicans and Puritans alike, both ecclesiastics and laymen, and the book was equally distasteful to the King. A particularly vicious onslaught was made by a Scottish divine, Samuel Rutherford, and it is pleasant to find that Milton, from the Puritan side of the political and theological fence, rushed to defend champions of tolerance in his poem, *On the New Forces of Conscience,* and is savagely indignant that men of "learning, faith, and pure intent" should be named heretics by a "Scotch What-d'ye-call."

In 1649 Taylor published *The Great Exemplar*, in which he puts aside controversies to compose a devout and simple life of Christ, the first of a long succession of such lives to be written in English in a popular style. It is evident with what relief Taylor turns from the angry polemics raging about him to write of his beloved Jesus. He confesses that he is "weary and toiled with rowing up and down in the seas of questions which the interests of Christendom have commenced."

And so he strings together a series of meditations on the narratives of Christ's life, in order, as he says, "to serve the purposes of religion by doing assistance to that part of theology which is wholly practical: that which makes us wiser, therefore, because it makes us better." He wishes to gain souls "not to a sect and a subdivision, but to the Christian religion." Toward this end is his excellent résumé of the stages and discipline of a contemplative's life, an account which is important because it shows the extent to which Taylor had already familiarized himself with mystical theology. The book is also of special interest because of his emphasis on Christ's humanity, although there is no thought of historical criticism: "The instances of His piety," Taylor writes, "were the actions of a very holy, but of an ordinary life. . . . He did so converse with men, that men, after that example, might forever converse with Him. . . . We are not commanded to imitate a life whose story tells of . . . abstractions of senses and immaterial transportations."

In its own day and for many years afterward *The Great Exemplar* was highly popular, yet its excessive length (over seven hundred closely printed pages) may well prove a deterrent to the modern reader.

The King, imprisoned for three years, was beheaded in 1649. A second edition of Taylor's *Apology for the Liturgy* appeared after the execution, with the daring dedication "to his most sacred Majesty." Meanwhile to escape persecution Taylor had found refuge with his influential patron Richard Vaughan, Earl of Carbery, a Churchman, but in good repute with the Puritans.

In Vaughan's estate, Golden Grove, situated in a romantic and isolated valley of South Wales, far from the sound of human voices raised in contention, Jeremy Taylor grew to be one of the greatest prose writers in England. It was within the Golden Grove period that he produced his *Holy Dying* and *A Yearly Course of Sermons,* and in lesser degree of excellence, the earlier *Holy Living.* In these he shows the astounding variety of his mind. At last the fruit of his tremendous reading comes pouring out; Greek philosophers, Latin historians and poets, the Church Fathers, all march across his pages. The most curious and bizarre stories rub shoulders with God-impelled flights of thought and with vivid and sensitive descriptions of external nature.

The *Holy Living* is perhaps the best known of Taylor's works; it is a book of practical instruction for members of the Church of England when its ministers were dispersed and its liturgy forbidden and indeed unheard, unless the services were carried out surreptiously in private houses. And so Taylor established rules for living, "plain, useful, and fitted for the best and worst understanding." There are also rules for the practice of prayer, which he calls "the ascent of the mind to God," reminders against temptation and impatience and "tediousness of spirit," all sound advice with emphasis on good works rather than on matters of creed.

Shortly after, Taylor was to voice the ancient truth that through suffering comes wisdom. Certainly it was not until he had experienced heavy sorrows that he reached his greatest heights as a writer. For the Countess of Carbery died, the first wife of the owner of Golden Grove, a lady to whose grace and goodness he owed much. There followed within a few months the death of his own wife. In *Holy Dying* Taylor faces death, without fear and squarely, its omnipresence and inevitability, and the uncertainty and shortness of life. "Death meets us everywhere," he says. "A man is a bubble . . . the dream of a shadow. . . . A man goes off and is forgotten, like the dream of a distracted person."

Holy Dying is a strange book. There is in its prose a sweep and grandeur which make it poetry, and a melancholy undercurrent like that in Ecclesiastes or Pindar or the Latin poets. On the other hand, the book is full of practical advice on how to prepare for death, and shows insight into the nature of sickness as well as of death itself.

Taylor hits upon the fact that sickness actually cures many "evils" of the spirit; sickness confines a man to "an inactive condition" and "takes away the sense of all the cross fortunes which amaze the spirits of some men and transport them certainly beyond all the limits of patience. . . . The fears of want and the troubles of ambition lie down and rest upon the sick man's pillow." In sickness, too, we are taken off from "the brisker relishes of the world," and the soul forgets its "knotty discourses" and "the spirit feels itself at ease."

His conception of death was not the customary one of his own day, the anthropomorphic figure waiting to strike man down. "Death," he maintains, "is not an action but a whole state and condition." And in his moving funeral sermon for the Countess of Carbery, he says that "death is nothing but a middle point between two lives." As such he would strip it of its conventional trappings. "Take away but the pomps of death, the disguises and solemn bugbears, the tinsel and the actings by candlelight, and proper and fantastic ceremonies, the minstrels and the noise-makers, the women and the weepers, the swoonings and the shriekings, the nurses and the physicians, the dark room and the ministers, the kindred and the watchers; and then to die is easy."

A wry humor crops up even here, at the deathbed: "A man at least gets this by death, that his calamities are not immortal." Taylor ridicules deathbed repentances as usually being too late; like washing, "it is cleanly and civil, but makes no change deeper than the skin"—one of his unorthodox views which caused him trouble.

"It is a great art," says Taylor, "to die well," an art one must learn in health while there is yet time. In fact time is the most precious thing we have: "This instant will never return again, and yet it may be this instant will declare or secure the fortune of a whole eternity."

As to the state after death, Taylor says we do not know. "It is ten to one but when we die we shall find the state of affairs wholly differing from all our opinions here, and that no man or sect hath guessed anything at all of it as it is."

Taylor is known to have been keenly interested in investigating reported cases of encounters with ghosts and to have given credence to at least one of them.[13] Yet in *Holy Dying* his warning is matter-of-fact: "If we think a ghost beholds us, it may be we have upon us the impressions likely to be made by love, and fear, and religion."

Taylor was chaplain at Golden Grove until probably about the beginning of 1655. In the sermons that he preached and later published in his *Course of Sermons for All the Sundays in the Year,* the masterful style and the beauty shown in the *Holy Dying* are sustained and given greater scope. There is, naturally, the added attraction of varied subject matter, making the *Course of Sermons* perhaps of all Taylor's writings the book that can be read in its entirety with the greatest pleasure.

Here are numerous descriptions, full of close observation and striking imagery, many of them obviously written in a state of rapture: dawn and larks soaring to heaven, "the falling stars and the little glow-worms of the world," the coming of spring and the waters that "melt with joy." In the sermon "The Marriage Ring," he is eloquent on the mysteries and pleasures of love. We read, too, his commonsense warnings against over-loquaciousness, a state in which mouths, like the gates of hell, are always open; and against overeating and drunkenness, a particularly caustic blast being reserved for the gastronomic excesses of the Royalists, who would offer their lives for a cause and yet could not resist gluttony and intemperance.

He dwells on the omnipresence of Christ, who died not a "single or a sudden death" but who dies forever "in all the sufferings of His servants." There are magnificent railings against lukewarmness in religion, advice to the searchers of truth not to choose a doctrine merely because they esteem the priest who holds it. He insists on the practical side of religion: "It is good to give to a church, but it is better to give to the poor." He has the courage to express the rare knowledge that no one sect holds the entire truth: "From every sect and community of Christians take anything that is good, that advances holy religion and the divine honour."

Through the varied pages, running like an undercurrent, there is always Taylor's love of God, His essence, His wisdom, His power; and there is Taylor's consciousness that God is reflected in the forces of nature and in the little creations of the earth, as well as, more clearly, in the actions of a holy life, "whereby God is pleased to glorify Himself." He is also "glorified" in the sun and moon, in the "rare fabric" of the honeycomb, in the "discipline" of bees, in the "economy" of ants, in the little houses of birds, in the "curiosity" of an eye—"God being pleased to delight in those little images and reflexes of Himself from those pretty mirrors, which, like a crevice in a wall, through a narrow perspective transmit the species of a vast excellency."

There are a few restrained references to mystical theology, probably few and restrained because, as Taylor had said in *The Liberty of Proph-*

esying, such secrets are "not to be understood" if offered to "public consideration." But seldom as Taylor mentions this phase of religion in his six thousand pages, we seem on those occasions to be very near the mainspring of his life. "When persons come to that height of grace, or contemplation rather, and they love God for Himself . . . all that is but heaven in another sense and under another name."

The charm of the *Sermons,* as well as of *Holy Dying,* lies partly in the fact that wisdom and common sense are interwoven in perfect naturalness and familiarity with fantastic *curiosa* and odds and ends of stories from the classics and other sources. We read of the unfortunate gentleman in Plutarch, suffering from a hangnail, and of the lady Fescennia who ate perfumed lozenges in the vain hope that the smell of wine should not predominate; there are casual references to Libyan tigers, Pannonian bears, Livinian sausages, Arcadian porter. Looking glasses in the temple at Smyrna depict the handsomest faces as deformed; old Lapland women dance fiercely and without joy; poor Livius Drusus never had play days or days of quiet when a boy; Fannius killed himself for fear of death; and the king of Parthia was a mole-catcher. A calm and cosmopolitan timelessness permeates these pages, and antiquity is made familiar. Young Scipio is a fool; there is an impost on Tragascan salt; old people near the Riphaean mountains are taught to discourse of death familiarly, as of a thing "that will certainly come, and ought so to do." And as for Taylor's readers, with him we " 'walk by the obelisk' and meditate in piazzas."

In the choice and combination of Taylor's words, there is at times a strange, almost surrealist dream-quality, as if the words themselves were self-propelled from his unconscious depths, occasionally stopping just this side of irrationality, never overstepping the line, always under control. As an example we read:

> "The attributes and acts of God sat at the foot of mercy, and all that mercy descended upon the head of man. For so the light of the world in the morning of the creation was spread abroad like a curtain, and dwelt no where, but filled the *expansum* with a dissemination great as the unfoldings of the air's looser garment, or the wilder fringes of the fire, without knots or order or combination. But God gathered the beams in His hand and united them into a globe of fire, and all the light of the world became the body of the sun; and He lent some to his weaker sister that walks in the night and guides a traveller, and teaches him to distinguish a house from a river, or a rock from a plain field. So is the mercy of God, a vast *expansum* and a huge ocean."

With all the fullness and freedom of creation which this passage evinces, it is clear that Taylor also exercised the critical faculty of a sound conscious mind that chose and discarded—two activities which many of our surrealist writers and painters today might do well to emulate. Taylor had the gift of inserting the stabilizing phrase.

In 1654 Taylor made frequent trips to London, and since he is known to have preached there in a church, the year was evidently marked by tolerance and laxity on the part of the Puritans. One of his auditors, fortunately for Taylor, was John Evelyn, that amiable and attractive gentleman who became Taylor's patron and friend, and whose house on the Thames, Sayes Court in Deptford, now part of London, was probably later to be an occasional refuge from persecution. Taylor became Evelyn's "ghostly father," and the friends conferred often concerning spiritual matters.

Through Evelyn's arrangement Taylor for a short time presumably lived in a house near London, where, as he says, he could enjoy the "advantages of society and bookes" that the city afforded. Until he left for Ireland he frequently visited Evelyn at Sayes Court, where many of the great minds of England met, among them the chemist and investigator of natural science, Robert Boyle.

The letters of Taylor and Evelyn for a period of six years are intimate and detailed. Taylor writes to Evelyn of many things: that he is "in some disorder by reason of the death of a little child of mine, a boy that lately made us very glad"; and a year later that he has buried "two sweet, hopeful boyes." He is rejoiced that Evelyn is in good health and still at liberty and that his piety has enabled him to "passe to greater degrees of . . . the love of God. It is the worke of your life, and I perceive you betake yourselfe heartily to it"—a remark that throws light on Evelyn's religious experience. "The soule returns to God," Taylor writes; "and that in no sense is death. . . . The soule desires to be re-united; and that which is dead desires not." His warmth and sensitivity are shown when he condoles with Evelyn on the "losse of that pretty person, your strangely hopeful boy." "Your dearest, strangest miracle of a boy", he later writes.

In the years from 1654 to 1658 Taylor's friends had frequent need to shield him as far as they were able from persecution. Unwisely he wrote an inflammatory preface to one of his books, published under the gracefully allusive title, *The Golden Grove.* The work in itself would otherwise have been innocuous, as it was merely an expansion of an earlier catechism for children. However, in the preface he rashly contrasts the Anglican form of church government with the Puritanic, and provocatively remarks, "but now . . . the people are fallen under the harrows and saws of impertinent and ignorant preachers, who think all religion is a sermon and all sermons ought to be libels against truth and old governors." Since Taylor also calls Cromwell by inference "the son of Zippor," it is not surprising that he was imprisoned, at least for a short time. There was at the moment a tendency on the part of the Parliamentarians to return to sterner measures; they forbade Anglican worship and suppressed the preachers. Taylor on this score alone would have been in danger, but thanks to Evelyn he was released from prison, Evelyn, as we have said, being one of the few who were in favor with both parties. One wonders, however, at Taylor's bad judgment and lack of consideration in calling attention to his patron, Lord Carbery, by using the name of his estate as the title of this antiparliamentarian tract.

Not long after the publication of *The Golden Grove,* Taylor was to run counter to his orthodox and influential Anglican associates, and on far more serious grounds. In his lengthy volume, *Unum Necessarium*, he expressed his own heterodox views on the controversial dogmas of original sin, free will, predestination, and deathbed repentances.

Taylor had previously consulted Duppa, Bishop of Salisbury, whom he revered, about the advisability of writing on the subject of repentance, the *unum necessarium* of salvation. Duppa had approved, never dreaming, as he later complained to his friend the Dean of Salisbury, that Taylor would "fall upon" the business of original sin. By the time the book was ready for the press, Taylor himself, in almost abject poverty, was imprisoned in Chepstow Castle. The reason for this fresh imprisonment, which lasted only about six months, is not known, but may well have been continued anger at the *Golden Grove* preface. Meanwhile the unsuspecting Bishop, eagerly reading some of the proof sent him by the publisher, had come upon what he called "the *coloquintida* that spoiled all the broth," the chapter on original sin. To his horror he found the book, whose publication he could not stop, teeming with Pelagian and Anabaptistic heresies on the subject of predestination.

Writing indignantly to Taylor, Duppa vigorously pointed out the scandal that his views would bring not only upon himself and upon "his poor desolate mother the church," but also upon "his grandmother the whole church of Christ." Remonstrances were in vain; "nothing could work upon him," the Bishop comments to the Dean of Salisbury. The printing went on with worse things to come, for Taylor conspicuously prefaced the book by a letter to Duppa and to Warner, Bishop of Rochester. He was "pleased," stormed Duppa, "to make use of my name in the very forehead of it." It is certainly difficult to understand Taylor's poor judgment, for the inscription, to all but Taylor himself, implied that the two bishops approved of his views.

Except for this needless affront, we admire the courage of Taylor, since to him exposure of the fallacy and the brutality of predestination, as he saw it, was a matter of conscience. He was in a position of influence and he felt that it would be cowardly not to set forth his views strongly. At least he had the satisfaction of knowing he had written convincingly, since Evelyn for one—and Taylor says there were many others—was a convert to his liberal reasoning.

But it is not surprising that the *Unum* brought on a storm that presumably affected the subsequent course of Taylor's life. Papists, Calvinists, and orthodox Anglicans were incensed by his heterodox stand. In a reply to a letter from Sheldon, Archbishop of Canterbury, advising him to recant his views, Taylor says that he is wearied from answering "particulars," reaffirms his loyalty to the Church of England, but flatly refuses to comply with his superior's request. "I may do weakly," he maintains, "but I cannot do unhandsome things."

The firmness with which Taylor held to his Arminian trends is evinced three years later by the books he chose for a list which in 1659, after he had settled in Ireland, he recommended to a theological library. In addition to seven volumes of his own he included the treatises of Episcopius, the great Arminian, "whose whole works," he comments, "are excellent, and containe the whole body of orthodox religion."

Heretical as Taylor appeared to the Archbishop of Canterbury, when we study his views as expressed in the *Unum*, we find that he does not deny original sin itself: Adam certainly sinned, he says, and passed on to his descendants the evils of sin, sorrow, lusts of the flesh, and mortality. But, Taylor argues, man can hardly be responsible for what is beyond his control; furthermore, "to deny to the will of man powers of choice and election, or the use of it in the actions of our life, destroys the immortality of the soul." "It is our own choice that we sin." Both God and man are necessary for man's salvation, he maintains. "Nature alone cannot bring us to God." "Eternal life . . . cannot be acquired by any natural means. . . . It is a gift . . . of God." On the other hand, over and over he says that "not God but ourselves are authors of our eternal death in case we do perish."

It is significant that several years before the *Unum*, in his *Course of Sermons* (Sermon III for the Summer Half-Year), Taylor had grappled with the ancient problem of original sin and its unjust consequences. "In sending evils upon the posterity of evil men," he wrote, "God serves many ends of providence, some of wisdom, some of mercy, some of justice, and contradicts none. . . . Our children, it may be, shall be sanctified by a sorrow, and purified by the power of affliction." This idea of purification and growth through suffering was Taylor's answer to the paradox of the justice of God and the suffering of the innocent.

For the most part, religions have rationalized the paradox by the supposition of an ancient curse, brought on by the sin of a primordial man, which works down the ages and causes the innocent descendants, as well as the evil, to suffer. We see this, for instance, in the Greek myths of Oedipus and Orestes as well as in the Hebrew *Genesis*. Now and then a lonely thinker, says Edith Hamilton,[11] has plumbed the problem more deeply. Such a man she finds, was Aeschylus, whose insight into the riddle of the world has not yet been superseded: Zeus "leadeth mortals the way of understanding" and "hath stablished as a fixed ordinance that 'wisdom cometh by suffering.' But even as trouble, bringing memory of pain, droppeth o'er the mind in sleep, so to those who would not, cometh wisdom."[12] Taylor's language in the passage quoted earlier does not breathe of the infinite as do the words of Aeschylus, but his meaning is much the same.

The times were becoming increasingly hard for Anglican clergy, since Cromwell, although tolerant toward most sects, was persecuting the Quakers and the Churchmen with severity. On Christmas Day, 1655, Evelyn records in his diary that in London he has heard the "funeral sermon of Preaching," this being the last day that a minister of the Church of England was allowed to preach or to administer the sacraments, "so that," he writes, "this was ye mournfullest day that in my life I had seene." Again in 1656 Evelyn is witness to the sad state of affairs in the Church: in a private house in London, he writes, he was given "the B. Sacrament, the first time the Church of England was reduced to a chamber and conventicle."

During much of this period, Taylor seems to have been officiating in private congregations, and probably had no settled abode and certainly no security. At least once more, in 1658, he was imprisoned, this time in the Tower of London, his offense being merely the use of a print of Christ in the attitude of prayer as the frontispiece to *A Collection of Offices,* which he had compiled as a substitute for the proscribed Book of Common Prayer. In fact, ever since he had left the enchanted shades of Golden Grove he had known poverty, criticism, confusion, and danger.

Through the influence of Evelyn, Taylor was again released from imprisonment, and a plan was shortly afterward formed by his friends to remove him from the perils of England. Edward, Earl of Conway, a loyal Anglican, had large estates in the northeast of Ireland; his residence was Portmore, eight miles from the town of Lisburn. Lord Conway considered Taylor "the choicest person in England appertaining to the conscience," and offered him a chaplainship. It was also suggested that Taylor share a lectureship in Lisburn with a Presbyterian, the stipend to be paid by private means.

Taylor disapproved of the plan at first, since it required, as he comments in a letter to Evelyn, that he serve "under the dispose of another," in a position where a Presbyterian and himself "shall be like Castor and Pollux, the one up and the other downe." The stipend also was inconsiderable, writes our divine, and moreover "the subscribers may die, or grow weary, or poore." But his objections were overcome; he had letters to important persons in Ireland, and a safe-conduct was given his family and himself by Cromwell.

And so in 1658 Taylor left his old friends, and the pleasant dinners with good minds at Sayes Court, and the crowds of London, the nerve-center of his world. For the rest of his life he was to live in a remote country. His homesickness for England is evident from his letters to Evelyn. "I pray say to me," he writes, "something concerning the state of learning; how is any art or science likely to improove? what good bookes are lately publicke?"

The Irish countryside was apparently as lovely in the seventeenth century as it is today. Taylor lived on a farm near his patron's mansion. Built after a plan by Inigo Jones, the great manor house must have delighted his keen senses. The desmesne of Portmore was washed by Lough Beg and Lough Neagh; on an island he could see a ruined monastery, and a tall round tower characteristic of the poetic Irish landscape. Not far off was the church where Taylor preached. The site as it appeared in 1904 has been gracefully described by Edmund Gosse.

"One arrives at last quite suddenly at its impressive desolation. It stands high on an artificial island in the marshes. . . . The fragments of the church are covered heavily with ivy, and a loose hedge of seedling larches and sweet-briar enrings them, while here and there great cypresses, relics, it is possible, of the Italian gardens of Portmore, soar impressively in the wild, bright place, where there has long ceased to be heard any other sound than the cries of wildfowl. From up among these ruins, the old fragmentary brickwork of Portmore is better visible than from any other point, and imagination may here rebuild the vision of it as Jeremy Taylor saw it when he arrived in 1658, sumptuous and elaborate, with its upper windows looking towards the sunset over Lough Beg to the melancholy little inland ocean of Lough Neagh."[14]

Such solitude would have been perfect for contemplation if only circumstances had been different. Unfortunately, ministers from the west of Scotland, representing the least educated and most embattled type of Presbyterians, filled the majority of the pulpits of Ulster and united to make the Englishman's life miserable. Any checkrein which might have been imposed on them by Cromwell was removed by his death in 1658, the year of Taylor's arrival. In the course of hostilities, a particularly embittered critic, Tandy, informed the privy council that the Anglican had used the sign of the cross in baptism. The harassed Churchman confides to Evelyn: "I feare my peace in Ireland is likely to be short, for a presbyterian and a madman have informed against me." On Tandy's information Taylor was arrested and sent to Dublin, but was shortly released, the atmosphere in the capital being less tense than in Ulster.

In 1660, probably in April, Taylor journeyed to London to see his friends and supervise the printing of his *Ductor Dubitantium.* Soon after, in May, came the Restoration, just in time for Taylor to dedicate this latest tome "To the most sacred Majesty of Charles II."

The great *Ductor* is a work which since Taylor's day has often been mentioned as one of the most important, although neglected, books of casuistry ever produced.[15] It covers 1,350 pages, more than one-fifth of Taylor's published writing, and had taken perhaps twenty years of time and labor. Since it was the work on which above all others Taylor seemed to think his fame would rest, he must have been disappointed by the coolness with which it was received during his lifetime. In 1660 people were much too excited by the Restoration and by hopes and fears for their own future to read such a weighty folio. Furthermore, the subject, cases of conscience and advice as to what should be done under a vast variety of circumstances, was already becoming outdated. But Taylor was a firm believer in the confessional, and had thought it a service to morality to gather together the fruits of his long experience as a spiritual adviser so that Anglicans, especially during the Protectorate, might have a guide in the absence of their confessors. With the Restoration and the return of Anglican clergy, there ceased to be any special need for Taylor's monumental work.

The *Ductor* shows as great zeal for compilation as we find in the huge compendiums of the Middle Ages. Taylor, however, deals with principles and codifies his cases as had not previously been done. Besides his rules for life, conduct, and the pursuit of God, there are precepts for the more extraordinary aspects of life. Do you want to marry your mother-in-law? Jeremy Taylor will tell you if you may. Should a preacher frighten his hearers with "panic terrors," informing them that if they are liars their faces will be deformed? Is one always bound to weep at the thought of one's sin? Here Taylor seems to say "no," although his thought is so overlaid with words, a trait unfortunately characteristic of the *Ductor,* that the anxious penitent might well be put to it to find the answer. Are duels lawful? Here there is a vigorous "no." Is it lawful for subjects to rebel? Again a firm "no," not on any pretext whatsoever. Must one fast in Lent? Fasting is all to the good, he says, but pharisaical fasting he abhors, and any law that requires little devices of superstition plays with "men's conscience as with a tennis-ball."

Indeed there is little from the cradle to the grave that Taylor does not discuss. But in spite of his often tiresome verbiage it must be said that he is always honest. Consider his words on mental reservation—which, incidentally, are quoted at length by Cardinal Newman, in defense of his own views, in the appendix to his *Apologia.* On this question, Taylor faces the fact that there are occasions in this imperfect world when speaking with mental reservations is almost essential. Thus he maintains that although to deceive is in general intrinsically evil, yet it is lawful to lie, for example, to save the life of a friend or a prince, or to circumvent an enemy. "Pretences . . . ought to serve the great end of charity," he says; and likewise physicians may lawfully lie to "hypochondriacal and disordered" persons to effect a cure. To sum up, Taylor says that we must not lie to God, "for God needs not a lie; but our brother does." And, we may add, it is equally clear that in not lying to God, Taylor could not lie to himself.

In its flashes of psychological insight the *Ductor* is one of the most astonishing of Taylor's books. On the question of scruples, for instance, he shows a knowledge of man's mind that anticipates modern study, his long experience as a confessor and spiritual guide doubtless having quickened his observation. His aim was evidently to liberate the penitent from the neurotic overscrupulousness that approaches the borderline of disease. "A scruple," he says, "is a great trouble of mind proceeding from a little motive and a great indisposition, by which the conscience though sufficiently determined by proper arguments dares not proceed to action; or if it do, it cannot rest." It is a "searching into little corners," a "fear of doing every thing that is innocent and an aptness to do every thing that can be suggested"; it may proceed from indisposition of body, sleepless nights, solitariness, "strong fancy and weak judgement."

Taylor knows also the mischief caused by nerves when a man is made fearful by a dream, or harassed by "the beating of a watch." His handling of such instances of neurosis speaks well for his helpfulness as a confessor.

In *The Worthy Communicant,* also published in 1660, Taylor states clearly his liberal position on several questions of doctrine. He believes that Christ is metaphysically but not corporally present in the Eucharist. He maintains that there is no magic in the sacrament itself: it will not make a man rich, or discover stolen goods, "or cure the tooth-ache." Moreover, "no grace is there improved but what we bring with us . . . we must come with charity, and we shall go away with more." *The Worthy Communicant* is written simply and soberly. We miss the raciness of expression and the elegance now almost forgotten. There are only a few flashes of epigram, such as, "Can a man bind a thought with chains, or carry imaginations in the palm of his hand?" And again, "Certain it is you will pray passionately if you desire fervently; prayers are but the body of the bird: desire are its angel's wings."

In 1661 Taylor was rewarded for his long devotion to his Church and his King by the bishoprics of Down and Connor. Why he was not recalled to England, as he had hoped, and to a see more in keeping with his talents, is not known, although his so-called "heresies" of denouncing predestination and the efficacy of deathbed repentances might well have lessened his chances of preferment. He was, however, appointed vice-chancellor of the University of Dublin, a position in which he did a prodigious amount of work in reorganization, the University's affairs having been left in disorder by the Civil War. He was also made a member of the Irish Privy Council.

Yet in spite of his new offices, Taylor, as we have said, continued to be unhappy in Ireland. Its climate disagreed with him and he was often ill; he was isolated from the world of literature and society that he loved. Although he had the companionship of Lord Conway whenever his new patron was in Ireland, he missed his friends in England, who gradually stopped writing.

The sharpest thorns in his flesh were still the Presbyterian ministers.[16] In the interim between his appointment as bishop and his consecration, he had invited these clergy to friendly conferences and called upon them personally. But their pulpits did not cease, as he says, to resound with invectives against Anglicans and Anglican liturgy, even with threats of bloodshed. The service book, the ministers told their congregations, was hatched in hell by the devil, and the Covenanters who first drew the bloody sword should draw it again before submitting to popish ceremonies. "They threaten to murder me," wrote Taylor in 1660 to the Duke of Ormonde, twice lord-lieutenant of Ireland; "I will petition your excellency to give me some parsonage in Munster."

We can understand the vehemence, though scarcely the cruelty, of the ministers, who felt that the salvation of souls depended on the promulgation of Calvinism; but in arguing that he was entitled to clergy that conformed to Anglican jurisdiction, Taylor would seem to have been within his rights. Since his opponents refused either to resign or to recognize his authority and continued to arouse dissension and incite their congregations to rebellion, Taylor, after he became bishop, summoned them to a conference in Lisburn. When only two out of their entire number complied, he declared thirty-six pulpits vacant, an action which has brought upon him a good deal of criticism.

Taylor's decisive stand did not secure lasting quiet in his diocese. In 1663 and again in 1667, just before his death, he writes of conspiracies and dissensions, a not unnatural result of this attempt to enforce in Ireland the Act of Uniformity, which forbade dissent from Episcopacy.

Harder to understand than Taylor's discharging of his Calvinistic clergy was his handling of the Irish Catholic peasantry within his diocese. The peasantry spoke no English, and according to him their priests did not allow them to learn it. Surely it is obvious that the Protestant clergy should under these circumstances have studied Gaelic. Bishop Bedell, thirty years earlier, had had the Bible translated into Gaelic, and by introducing services in that language had won the respect of the people. But the much-traveled Bedell had lived four years in Venice as chaplain to the English ambassador, and had been taught Italian by his friend Father Paul Sarpi; he therefore knew at first hand the inestimable advantage of conversing with a man in a common tongue, especially that in which the man was born. By speaking Gaelic to the peasants, the Anglican clergy under Bedell were better able to meet the needs of their congregations.

But Taylor and the other Churchmen of his time compelled the Irish to listen to sermons in a language they did not understand. Tactlessly also, though from conscientious motives, Taylor brought out his lengthy *Dissuasive from Popery,* which speaks of the "poor deluded Irish" and shows appreciation neither of the Celtic race and its innate religious bent, nor of those aspects of the Roman faith which were sympathetic to the Irish temperament. He saw only the abuses of popery and denounced the hold of the priesthood on the country.

Taylor's writings in Ireland are relatively unimportant, with the exception of several glorious sermons, among them the one preached in 1662 to the scholars of "the little but excellent university" of Dublin, a profound piece of writing, at once exciting and spiritual. Perhaps he was inspired by an audience of young people "whose business is to study for truth"—a grateful contrast to the rigid minds he had been combatting through so much of his life.

In his latter years Taylor was irritable, crushed with ill health and perpetual plotting against the Anglican Church, and hardened by his attempt to enforce the Act of Uniformity. For many years he must have had to bear yet another sort of bitterness—the loss of six sons. His only other boy, the intimate friend of the dissolute Duke of Buckingham, had suffered from a prolonged illness and was buried less than two weeks after his father.

Taylor died probably at the age of fifty-four. It is sad to contemplate the last years of this ardent man of genius, who had spent his life in the service of that "great family of God, the world." He deserved better of fate than to live so long in a situation which, considering his temperament, was almost intolerable. As he himself might have said, "It was gravel in the teeth."

JEREMY TAYLOR

Engraved by H. Adlard from an original painting of unknown authorship in the Hall of All Souls College, Oxford

SELECTIONS

He was a person of great humility; and notwithstanding his stupendous parts, and learning, and eminency of place, he had nothing in him of pride . . . but was courteous and affable, and of easy access, and would lend a ready ear to the complaints, yea to the impertinencies, of the meanest persons. . . . I believe he spent the greatest part of his time in heaven . . . and frequent aspirations and emigrations of his soul after God made up the best part of his devotions. But he was not only a good man God-ward, but . . . to all his other virtues added a large and diffusive charity.

George Rust, Bishop of Dromore
From *A Funeral Sermon,* preached
at the obsequies of Jeremy Taylor

Key to Abbreviation of Titles

D.I.O.M. .... *The Divine Institution of the Office Ministerial.*
D.J. .... *Deus Justificatus.*
D.P. .... *A Dissuasive from Popery.*
Ductor .... *Ductor Dubitantium.*
F.C.C. .... *A Funeral Sermon Preached at the Obsequies of the Countess of Carbery.*
F.G.D. .... *A Sermon Preached at the Funeral of that Worthy Knight, Sir George Dalstone.*
F.L.P. .... *A Sermon Preached at the Funeral of the Lord Primate.*
G.E. .... *The Great Exemplar.*
H.D. .... *The Rule and Exercise of Holy Dying.*
H.D.D. .... *The Rule and Exercise of Holy Dying,* the dedication.
H.L. .... *The Rule and Exercise of Holy Living.*
H.L.D. .... *The Rule and Exercise of Holy Living,* the dedication.
L.P. .... *The Liberty of Prophesying.*
L.P.D. .... *The Liberty of Prophesying,* the dedication.
M.D. .... *The Minister's Duty in Life and Doctrine.*
M.F. .... *The Measures and Offices of Friendship.*
S.F.L. .... *An Apology for Authorized and Set Forms of the Liturgy.*
S.G.H. .... *A Sermon: The Gate to Heaven a Strait Gate.*
S.P. .... *A Sermon Preached at the Opening of the Parliament of Ireland.*
S.S. .... *A Course of Sermons for the Summer Half-Year.*
S.S.D. .... *A Course of Sermons for the Summer Half-Year,* the dedication.
S.W. .... *A Course of Sermons for the Winter Half-Year.*
Un.D. .... *A Sermon Preached to the University of Dublin.*
Unum .... *Unum Necessarium.*
W. .... *A Letter to Bishop Warner.*
Wor. Com. ..... *The Worthy Communicant.*

For the convenience of the reader these selections from Jeremy Taylor have been grouped under general headings. The punctuation has been occasionally modernized and Greek or Latin phrases usually have been omitted without indication when the translation is given. The selections have been taken from the ten-volume edition of Jeremy Taylor's works edited by Reginald Heber, revised by Charles Page Eden and Alexander Taylor, and printed by Longman, Brown, Green, and Longman (London, 1850-59). *The volume and page given after each excerpt refer to this edition.*

TOLERANCE AND LIBERTY OF THOUGHT

While men contend for truth, error, dressed in the same habit, slips into her chair, and all the litigants court her for the divine sister of wisdom; there is noise but no harmony, fighting but no victory, talking but no learning: all are teachers, and all are willful, every man is angry, and without reason and without charity. *S.W. (xxiii); IV, 296.*

Such being the nature of men, that they think it the greatest injury in the world when other men are not of their minds; and that they please God most when they are most furiously zealous, and no zeal better to be expressed than by hating all those whom they are pleased to think God hates. *G.E. (Pt. ii, § xii); II, 329.*

For if it be evinced that one heaven shall hold men of several opinions, if the unity of faith be not destroyed by that which men call differing religions, and if an unity of charity be the duty of us all, even towards persons that are not persuaded of every proposition we believe, then I would fain know to what purpose are all those stirs and great noises in Christendom. . . .

All these mischiefs proceed not from this, that all men are not of one mind, for that is neither necessary nor possible; but that every opinion is made an article of faith, every article is a ground of a quarrel, every quarrel makes a faction, every faction is zealous, and all zeal pretends for God, and whatsoever is for God cannot be too much: we by this time are come to that pass, we think we love not God except we hate our brother, and we have not the virtue of religion unless we persecute all religions but our own. *L.P.; V, 367 f.*

When interest divides the church and the calentures of men breathe out in problems and inactive discourses, each part, in pursuance of its own portion, follows that proposition which complies with and bends in all the flexures of its temporal ends. And while all strive for truth, they hug their own opinions dressed up in her imagery and they dispute forever; and either the question is indeterminable or, which is worse, men will never be convinced. For such is the nature of disputings that they begin commonly in mistakes, they proceed with zeal and fancy, and end not at all but in schisms and uncharitable names, and too often dip their feet in blood. . . .

I have chosen to serve the purposes of religion by doing assistance to that part of theology which is wholly practical; that which makes us wiser, therefore, because it makes us better. And truly, my lord [Lord Hatton], it is enough to weary the spirit of a disputer that he shall argue till he hath lost his voice and his time, and sometimes the question too, and yet no man shall be of his mind more than was before. How few turn Lutherans, or Calvinists, or Roman Catholics, from the religion either of their country or interest! Possibly two or three . . . pass from church to church, upon grounds as weak as those for which formerly they did dissent. . . . But he that follows the work of God, that is, labors to gain souls not to a sect and a subdivision but to the Christian religion . . . hath a promise to be assisted and rewarded: and all those that go to heaven are the purchase of such undertakings, the fruit of such culture and labours; for it is only a holy life that lands us there.

And now, my lord . . . I shall not be ashamed to say that I am weary and toiled with rowing up and down in the seas of questions which the interests of Christendom have commenced. *G.E.D.; II, 1 ff.*

The truth is . . . men do not learn their doctrines from scripture, but come to the understanding of scripture with preconceptions and ideas of doctrines of their own. And then no wonder that scriptures look like pictures wherein every man in the room believes they look on him only, and *that* wheresoever he stands or how often soever he changes his station. . . . There are sixteen several opinions concerning original sin; and as many definitions of the sacraments as there are sects of men that disagree about them.

And now what help is there for us in the midst of these uncertainties? If we follow any one translation or any one man's commentary, what rule shall we have to choose the right by? Or is there any one man that hath translated perfectly or expounded infallibly? No translation challenges such a prerogative to be authentic but the Vulgar Latin; and yet see with what good success: for when it was declared authentic by the Council of Trent, Sixtus put forth a copy much mended of what it was and tied all men to follow that. But that did not satisfy; for Pope Clement reviews and corrects it in many places, and still the decree remains in a changed subject. *L.P.; V, 426.*

The infinite variety of opinions in matters of religion . . . have . . . caused great divisions of the heart and variety of thoughts and designs amongst pious and prudent men. . . . Some have endeavoured to reunite these fractions by propounding such a guide which they were all bound to follow, hoping that the unity of a guide would have persuaded unity of minds; but who this guide should be at last became such a question that it was made part of the fire that was to be quenched, so far was it from extinguishing any part of the flame. Others thought of a rule, and this must be the means of union, or nothing could do it. But supposing all the world had been agreed of this rule, yet the interpretation of it was so full of variety that this also became part of the disease for which the cure was pretended. All men resolved upon this, that though they yet had not hit upon the right, yet some way must be thought upon to reconcile differences in opinion. . . . Few men in the meantime considered that so long as men had such variety of principles, such several constitutions, educations, tempers and distempers, hopes, interests, and weaknesses, degrees of light and degrees of understanding, it was impossible all should be of one mind; and what is impossible to be done, is not necessary it should be done. . . . Although the Spirit of God did rest upon us in divided tongues, yet so long as those tongues were of fire, not to kindle strife but to warm our affections and inflame our charities, we should find that this variety of opinions in several persons would be looked upon as an argument only of diversity of operations, while the Spirit is the same.

L.P.; V, 365 f.

Some very wise men . . . have undertaken to reconcile the differences of Christendom by a way of moderation. Thus they have projected to reconcile the Papists and the Lutherans, the Lutherans and the Calvinists, the remonstrants and contra-remonstrants, and project that each side should abate of their asperities and pare away something of their propositions, and join in common terms and phrases of accommodation, each of them sparing something, and promising they shall have a great deal of peace. . . . This was the way of . . . Erasmus, Spalato, Grotius, and indeed of Charles the fifth in part, but something more heartily of Ferdinand the second. This device produced the conferences at Poissy, at Montpellier, at Ratisbon, at the Hague, at many places more; and what was the event of these? Their parties when their delegates returned either disclaimed their moderation, or their respective princes had some other ends to serve. . . .

And what is now to be done? Must truth be forever in the dark, and the world forever be divided, and societies disturbed, and governments weakened, and our spirits debauched with error and the uncertain opinions and the pedantry of talking men? . . . But the way hath not yet been hit upon. . . . You look for it in your books, and you tug hard for it in your disputations, and you derive it from the cisterns of the fathers, and you enquire after the old ways, and sometimes are taken with new appearances, and you rejoice in false lights, or are delighted with little umbrages and peep of day. . . . We have examined all ways but one, all but God's way. Let us (having missed in all the other) try this: let us go to God for truth . . . if we miss the truth it is because we will not find it. . . .

My text is simple as truth itself. . . . The way to judge of religion is by doing of our duty; and theology is rather a divine life than a divine knowledge. In heaven indeed we shall first see, and then love; but here on earth we must first love, and love will open our eyes as well as our hearts, and we shall then see and perceive and understand.

Un. D.; VIII, 365-68.

Men are now-a-days . . . so in love with their own fancies and opinions as to think faith and all christendom is concerned in their support and maintenance; and whoever is not so fond and does not dandle them like themselves, it grows up to a quarrel, which, because it is *in materia theologiae,* is made a quarrel in religion, and God is entitled to it; and then if you are once thought an enemy to God, it is our duty to persecute you even to death; . . . perhaps when all comes to all, it is a false opinion or a matter of human interest, that we have so zealously contended for; for to one of these heads most of the disputes of christendom may be reduced. . . . It is not the differing opinions that is the cause of the present ruptures, but want of charity; it is not the variety of understandings, but the disunion of wills and affections; it is not the several principles, but the several ends, that cause our miseries.

L.P.; V, 367.

The fault I find, and seek to remedy, is that men are so dogmatical and resolute in their opinions, and impatient of others' disagreeings in those things wherein is no sufficient means of union and determination; but that men should let opinions and problems keep their own forms and not be obtruded as axioms. . . .

Since there are and ever were and ever will be variety of opinions, because there is variety of human understandings and uncertainty in things, no man should be too forward in determining all questions, nor so forward in prescribing to others, nor invade that liberty which God hath left to us entire, by propounding many things obscurely.

L.P.D.; V, 346 f.

There is no church that is in prosperity but alters her doctrine every age, either by bringing in new doctrines or by contradicting her old; which shews that none are satisfied with themselves or with their own confessions. And since all churches believe themselves fallible (that only excepted which all other churches say is most of all deceived), it were strange if in so many articles which make up their several bodies of confessions they had not mistaken every one of them in something or other. The Lutheran churches maintain consubstantiation, the Zuinglians are sacramentaries, the Calvinists are fierce in the matters of absolute predetermination, and all these reject episcopacy, which the primitive church would have made no doubt to have called heresy. The Socinians profess a portentous number of strange opinions; they deny the holy Trinity . . . the Anabaptists laugh at Paedo-baptism; the Ethiopian churches are Nestorian. Where then shall we fix our confidence or join communion? To pitch upon any one of these is to throw the dice if salvation be to be had only in one of them; and that every error that by chance hath made a sect and is distinguished by a name be damnable.

If this consideration does not deceive me, we have no other help in the midst of these distractions and disunions, but all of us to be united in that common term . . . the Creed of the Apostles; and in all other things an honest endeavour to find out what truths we can, and a charitable and mutual permission to others that disagree from us and our opinions. I am sure this may satisfy us, for it will secure us; but I know not any thing else that will. *L.P.D.; V, 356 f.*

If the apostles admitted all to their communion that believed this creed, why shall we exclude any that preserve the same entire? *L.P.; V, 373.*

When good men pray with one heart and in a holy assembly, that is, holy in their desires, lawful in their authority, though the persons be of different complexions: then the prayer flies up to God like the hymns of a choir of angels; for God . . . loves that His church should imitate the concords of heaven and the unions of God. *S.W. (v); IV, 69.*

From every sect and community of Christians take anything that is good, that advances holy religion and the divine honour. For one hath a better government, a second a better confession, a third hath excellent spiritual arts for the conduct of souls, a fourth hath fewer errors. And by what instrument soever a holy life is advantaged, use that, though thou grindest thy spears and arrows at the forges of the Philistines, knowing thou hast no master but Christ, no religion but the Christian, no rule but the scriptures and the laws and right reason. *S.S. (xxii); IV, 607.*

I consider that there are but few doctrines of christianity that were ordered to be preached to all the world, to every single person, and made a necessary article of his explicit belief. *L.P.D.; V, 348.*

If I shall tie other men to believe my opinion because I think I have a place of scripture which seems to warrant it to my understanding, why may he not serve up another dish to me in the same dress, and exact the same task of me to believe the contradictory? . . . For it is a hard case that we should think all papists, and anabaptists, and sacramentaries, to be fools and wicked persons: certainly among all these sects there are very many wise men and good men, as well as erring. And although some zeals are so hot and their eyes so inflamed with their ardours that they do not think their adversaries look like other men, yet certainly we find by the results of their discourses and the transactions of their affairs of civil society, that they are men that speak and make syllogisms, and use reason, and read scripture. *L.P.D.; V, 345.*

I suppose skill in controversies (as they are now used) to be the the worst part of learning, and time is the worst spent in them, and men the least benefited by them—that is, when the questions are curious and impertinent [not pertinent], intricate and unexplicable, not to make men better, but to make a sect. But when the propositions disputed are of the foundation of faith, or lead to good life, or naturally do good to single persons or public societies, then they are part of the *depositum* of Christianity . . . and therefore controversies may become necessary; but because they are not often so, but oftentimes useless and always troublesome; and as an ill diet makes an ill habit of body, so does the frequent use of controversies baffle the understanding, and makes it crafty to deceive others, itself remaining instructed in nothing but useless notions and words of contingent signification and distinctions without difference, which minister to pride and contention and teach men to be pertinacious, troublesome, and uncharitable; therefore I love them not.

D.P. (Pt. i, pref.); VI, 173.

For my own particular, I cannot but expect that God in His justice should enlarge the bounds of the Turkish empire, or some other way punish Christians, by reason of their pertinacious disputing about things unnecessary, undeterminable, and unprofitable, and for their hating and persecuting their brethren, which should be as dear to them as their own lives, for not consenting to one another's follies and senseless vanities. How many volumes have been writ about angels, about immaculate conception, about original sin, when all that is solid reason or clear revelation in all these three articles may be reasonably enough comprised in forty lines?

L.P.D.; V, 361 f.

A good man that believes what according to his light . . . he thinks true, whether he hits upon the right or no, because he hath a mind desirous of truth, and prepared to believe every truth, is therefore acceptable to God because nothing hindered him from it but what he could not help.

L.P.; V, 397.

I earnestly contend that another man's opinion shall be no rule to mine, and that my opinion shall be no snare and prejudice to myself; that men use one another so charitably and so gently that no error or violence tempt men to hypocrisy. . . .

If men would not call all opinions by the name of religion, and superstructures by the name of fundamental articles, and all fancies by the glorious appellative of faith, this objection would have no pretense or footing. . . . We may as well decree a wart to be mortal, as a various opinion to be capital and damnable. *L.P.; V, 348.*

The painter that exposed his work to the censure of the common passengers, resolving to mend it as long as any man could find fault, at last had brought the eyes to the ears and the ears to the neck, and for his excuse subscribed, *Hanc populus fecit;* but his *hanc ego,* that which he made by the rules of his art and the advice of men skilled in the same mystery, was the better piece. The Church of England should have pared away all the canon of the communion if she had mended her piece at the prescription of the Zuinglians, and all her office of baptism if she had mended by the rules of the Anabaptists, and kept up altars still by the example of the Lutherans, and not have retained decency [appropriateness?] by the good will of the Calvinists.

S.F.L. (*pref.*); *V, 235.*

Since . . . there are in scripture many other mysteries and matters of question upon which there is a veil . . . he that is the wisest . . . will be very far from confidence. . . . And therefore a wise man that considers this would not willingly be prescribed to by others, and therefore if he also be a just man he will not impose upon others; for it is best every man should be left in that liberty from which no man can justly take him. *L.P.; V, 427 f.*

Whatever ye do, let not the pretense of a different religion make you think it lawful to oppress any man in his just rights . . . to do right to them that are of another opinion is the way to win them; but if you for conscience sake do them wrong, they will hate you and your religion.

S.P.; VIII, 357.

Let them [the governors] remember but the gentleness of Christianity, the liberty of consciences which ought to be preserved, and let them do justice to the persons whoever they are that are peevish, provided no man's person be overborne with prejudice. For if it be necessary for all men to subscribe to the present established religion, by the same reason at another time a man may be bound to subscribe to the contradictory, and so to all religions in the world. . . .

If you persecute heretics or discrepants they unite themselves as to a common defence. If you permit them, they divide themselves upon private interests. *L.P.; V, 535 f.*

And indeed there is great reason for princes to give toleration to disagreeing persons whose opinions by fair means cannot be altered. For if the persons be confident [secure?] they will serve God according to their persuasions; and if they be publicly prohibited, they will privately convene. *L.P.D.; V, 351.*

The ecclesiastical power . . . is not of capacity to use the temporal sword or corporal inflictions. The mere doctrines and opinions of men are things spiritual, and therefore not cognoscible by a temporal authority.

And the ecclesiastical authority which is to take cognizance is itself so spiritual that it cannot inflict any punishment corporal. *L.P.; V, 596.*

What that unity and universality is (which can be introduced by force) a great part of the world hath had too long an experience to be ignorant. *Ductor* (*Bk. ii, ch. iii*); *IX, 630.*

We must not quickly, nor upon slight grounds, nor unworthy instances, call heretic. There had need be a long process and a high conviction and a competent judge and a necessary article, that must be ingredients into . . . condemnation of a person or opinion. . . .

It were well we were not so forward to refuse communion with dissenting persons, upon the easy and confident mistakes of a too forward zeal. They that call heretic may themselves be the mistaken persons and . . . may shut their doors upon truth and their windows against light and refuse to let salvation in. *G.E.* (*Pt. ii, § xii*); *II, 339.*

Heresy is not an error of the understanding, but an error of the will.
No man is a heretic against his will. *L.P.; V, 382, 386.*

I would fain know, why is not any vicious habit as bad or worse than a false opinion? Why are we so zealous against those we call heretics, and yet great friends with drunkards, fornicators, and swearers, and intemperate and idle persons! . . . I am certain that a drunkard is as contrary to God and lives as contrary to the laws of Christianity as a heretic; and I am also sure that I know what drunkenness is: but I am not sure that such an opinion is heresy. *L.P.D.; V, 359.*

A holy life will make our belief holy, if we consult not humanity and its imperfections in the choice of our religion, but search for truth without designs save only of acquiring heaven, and then be as careful to preserve charity as we were to get a point of faith. *L.P.D.; V, 367.*

If any man differs from me in opinion, I am not troubled at it, but tell him that truth is in the understanding and charity is in the will, and is or ought to be there before either his or my opinion in these controversies can enter; and therefore that we ought to love alike though we do not understand alike. *D.J.* (*pref.*); *VII, 495.*

Boldness of assertion, except it be in matters of faith and clearest revelation, is an argument of the vanity of the man, never of the truth of the proposition: for to such matters the saying of Xenophanes in Varro, is pertinent and applicable, "God only knows them, and we conjecture."

And although I be as desirous to know what I should and what I should not, as any of my brethren the sons of Adam; yet I find that the more I search, the further I am from being satisfied, and make but few discoveries save of my own ignorance. *L.P.D.; V, 363.*

Since no church of one name is infallible, a wise man may have . . . a reason to believe of every one in particular that she errs in some article or other. . . . What is it to me if the Greek church denies procession of the third Person from the second, so she will give me the right hand of fellowship though I affirm it, therefore because I profess the religion of Jesus Christ? *L.P.; V, 603.*

I end with a story which I find in the Jews' books.* "When Abraham sat at his tent-door, according to his custom, waiting to entertain strangers, he espied an old man stooping and leaning on his staff, weary with age and travel, coming towards him, who was a hundred years of age. He received him kindly, washed his feet, provided supper, caused him to sit down; but observing that the old man eat and prayed not, nor begged for a blessing on his meat, he asked him why he did not worship the God of heaven: the old man told him that he worshipped the fire only, and acknowledged no other god. At which Abraham grew so zealously angry that he thrust the old man out of his tent, and exposed him to all the evils of the night and an unguarded condition. When the old man was gone, God called to Abraham, and asked him where the stranger was; he replied, 'I thrust him away because he did not worship Thee.' God answered him, 'I have suffered him these hundred years, although he dishonored Me, and couldst not thou endure him one night, when he gave thee no trouble?' Upon this," saith the story, "Abraham fetched him back again and gave him hospitable entertainment and wise instruction." Go thou and do likewise, and thy charity will be rewarded by the God of Abraham. *L.P.; V, 604 f.*

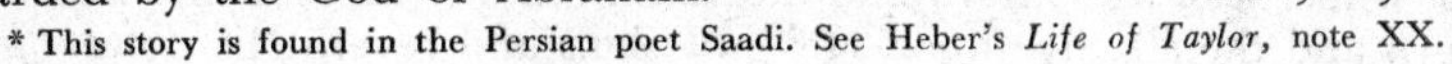

* This story is found in the Persian poet Saadi. See Heber's *Life of Taylor,* note XX.

THE NATURE OF GOD

God is wholly in every place, included in no place; not bound with cords except those of love; not divided into parts, not changeable into several shapes; filling heaven and earth with His present power, and with His never absent nature: so St. Augustine expresses this article. So that we may imagine God to be as the air and the sea, and we all enclosed in His circle, wrapped up in the lap of His infinite nature, or as infants in the wombs of their pregnant mothers: and we can no more be removed from the presence of God than from our own being. . . .

God is present by His essence, which, because it is infinite, cannot be contained within the limits of any place; and because He is of an essential purity and spiritual nature, He cannot be undervalued by being supposed present in the places of unnatural uncleanness: because as the sun, reflecting upon the mud of strands and shores, is unpolluted in its beams, so is God not dishonoured when we suppose Him in every of His creatures, and in every part of every one of them, and is still as unmixt with any unhandsome adherence as is the soul in the bowels of the body.

God is everywhere present by His power. He rolls the orbs of heaven with His hand; He fixes the earth with His foot; He guides all the creatures with His eye, and refreshes them with His influence. He makes the powers of hell to shake with His terrors, and binds the devils with His word and throws them out with His command; and sends the angels on embassies with His decrees. He hardens the joints of infants, and confirms the bones when they are fashioned beneath secretly in the earth. He it is that assists at the numerous productions of fishes; and there is not one hollowness in the bottom of the sea but He shews Himself to be Lord of it, by sustaining there the creatures that come to dwell in it: and in the wilderness, the bittern and the stork, the dragon and the satyr, the unicorn and the elk, live upon His provisions and revere His power, and feel the force of His almightiness. *H.L. (ch. i); III, 23.*

That great wise Dispenser of all things in heaven and earth, who makes twins in the little continent of their mother's womb to lie at ease and peace; and the eccentric motions of the orbs, and the regular and irregular progressions of the stars not to cross or hinder one another; and in all the variety of human actions, cases and contingencies—hath so wisely disposed His laws that no contradiction of chance can infer a contradiction of duty. *Ductor (Bk. iii, ch. iii); X, 248.*

Nathanael's faith was produced by an argument not demonstrative, not certainly concluding; Christ knew him when He saw him first, and he believed Him to be the Messias. His faith was excellent, whatever the argument was. And I believe a God, because the sun is a glorious body; or because of the variety of plants, or the fabric and rare contexture of a man's eye: I may as fully assent to the conclusion as if my belief dwelt upon the demonstrations made by the prince of philosophers in the eighth of his physics and twelfth of his metaphysics.

G.E. (*Pt. ii*, § *x*); *II, 294.*

In the first [commandment], the unity of the Godhead is expressly affirmed; in the second, His invisibility and immateriality; in the third is affirmed God's government and providence . . . in the fourth commandment He proclaims Himself the Maker of heaven and earth . . . and consequently to this, it also was a confession of His goodness, His omnipotence, and His wisdom—all which were written with a sunbeam in the great book of the creature. *H.L.* (*ch. iv*); *III, 171.*

The grace of God is like a graff put into a stock of another nature; it makes use of the faculties and juice of the stock and natural root, but converts all into its own nature. *Unum* (*ch. v*); *VII, 189.*

God's works are secret, and His words are deep, and His dispensations mysterious, and therefore too high for thy understanding. S. Gregory Nazianzen says of God, "The more you think you comprehend of Him in your understanding, the less He is comprehended"; like the sand of the glass which the harder you grasp the less you can retain; or like the sand of the sea which you can never number.

Wor. Com. (*ch. iii*); *VIII, 107.*

The Jews have a saying: he that will understand God's meaning must look above and below, and round about; for the meaning of the Spirit of God is not like the wind blowing from one point, but like light issuing from the body of the sun; it is light round about. And in every word of God there is a treasure, and something will be found somewhere to answer every doubt and to clear every obscurity, and to teach every truth by which God intends to perfect our understandings. But then, take this rule with you: do not pass from plainness to obscurity, nor from simple principles draw crafty conclusions, nor from easiness pass into difficulty, nor from wise notices draw intricate nothings, nor from the wisdom of God lead your hearers into the follies of men.

M.D.; VIII, 529.

We may sit down and reckon by great sums and conjugations of His gracious gifts, and tell the minutes of eternity by the number of the divine mercies. . . . His mercies make contemptible means instrumental to great purposes and a small herb the remedy of the greatest diseases. He impedes the devil's rage and infatuates his counsels; He diverts his malice and defeats his purposes; He binds him in the chain of darkness and gives him no power over the children of light; He suffers him to talk in solitary places and yet fetters him that he cannot disturb the sleep of a child; He hath given him mighty power and yet a young maiden that resists him shall make him flee away. . . . He gave him power over the winds and made him prince of the air, and yet the breath of a holy prayer can drive him as far as the utmost sea. And He hath so restrained him that, except it be by faith, we know not whether there be any devil, yea or no, for we never heard his noises nor have seen his affrighting shapes. *S.S. (xxvii); IV, 661.*

We believe a story which we love, taking probabilities for demonstrations and casual accidents for probabilities: and anything creates vehement presumptions, in which cases our guides are not our knowing faculties but our affections. And if they be holy, God guides them into the right persuasions as He does little birds to make rare nests, though they understand not the mystery of operation nor the design and purpose of the action. *G.E. (Pt. ii, § x); II, 286.*

Since to God all matter is alike and no more accrues to Him in a hecatomb than a piece of gum, in an ascetic severity than in a secular life, God regards not the matter of a precept but the obedience, which in all instances is the same. *G.E. (Pt. i, § v); II, 111.*

God understands the priest's thoughts when he speaks not, as well as when he speaks. He hears the prayer of the heart, and sees the word of the mind. . . . A man who understands not what is said can only pray with his lips, for the heart cannot pray but by desiring and it cannot desire what it understands not. *D.P. (Pt. i, ch. i); VI, 212.*

All the treasures of God which are in the psalms are my own riches and the wealth of my hope: there will I look, and whatsoever I can need, that I will depend upon. For certainly, if we could understand it, that which is infinite (as God is) must needs be some such kind of thing: it must go whither it was never sent, and signify what was not first intended; and it must warm with its light and shine with its heat, and refresh when it strikes, and heal when it wounds, and ascertain where it makes afraid, and intend all when it warns one, and mean a great deal in a small word. And as the sun, passing to its southern tropic, looks with an open eye upon his sun-burnt Ethiopians, but at the same time sends light from its posterns and collateral influences from the back-side of his beams, and sees the corners of the east when his face tends toward the west, because he is a round body of fire, and hath some little images and resemblances of the Infinite: so is God's mercy. When it looked upon Moses it relieved St. Paul, and it pardoned David, and gave hope to Manasses, and might have restored Judas, if he would have had hope and used himself accordingly. *H.D. (ch. v); III, 431.*

To revenge it [a sin] forever, upon all generations and with an eternal anger upon some persons, even the most innocent, cannot without trembling be spoken or imagined of God, who is the great lover of souls.
Unum (ch. vi); VII, 270.

Can anything in this world be more foolish than to think that all this rare fabric of heaven and earth can come by chance, when all the skill of art is not able to make an oyster? To see rare effects, and no cause; an excellent government, and no prince; a motion without an immovable; a circle, without a center; a time without eternity; a second without a first; a thing that begins not from itself, and therefore not to perceive there is something from whence it does begin, which must be without beginning: these things are so great against philosophy and natural reason that he must needs be a beast in his understanding that does not assent to them. This is the atheist; the tongue never made itself to speak, and yet talks against Him that did, saying, that which is made, is, and that which made it, is not. *S.W. (xx); IV, 249 f.*

God hath no shape or form, and therefore these fathers could not speak against making images of a thing that was not; and as for the images of His essence, no Christian, no heathen ever pretended to it; and no man or beast can be pictured so: no painter can paint an essence.
D.P. (Bk. ii, § vii); VI, 640.

Do not think that God is only to be found in a great prayer or a solemn office: He is moved by a sigh, by a groan, by an act of love.
H.D. (ch. iv); III, 357.

You may as well measure eternity with a span and grasp an infinite in the palm of your hand, as draw the circles and depict Him that hath no colour or figure, no parts nor body, no accidents nor visibility.
Ductor (Bk. ii, ch. ii); IX, 420.

The attributes and acts of God sat at the foot of mercy, and all that mercy descended upon the head of man. For so the light of the world in the morning of the creation was spread abroad like a curtain, and dwelt nowhere, but filled the *expansum* with a dissemination great as the unfoldings of the air's looser garment, or the wilder fringes of the fire, without knots, or order, or combination; but God gathered the beams in His hand and united them into a globe of fire, and all the light of the world became the body of the sun; and He lent some to his weaker sister that walks in the night, and guides a traveler, and teaches him to distinguish a house from a river, or a rock from a plain field. So is the mercy of God, a vast *expansum* and a huge ocean; from eternal ages it dwelt round about the throne of God, and it filled all that infinite distance and space that hath no measures but the will of God.

S.S. (xxv); IV, 633.

FREE WILL VERSUS PREDESTINATION

The will is the mistress of all our actions, of all but such as are necessary and natural; and therefore to her it is to be imputed whatsoever is done. The action itself is good or bad by its conformity to or difformity from the rule of conscience; but the man is good or bad by the will. . . .

We are sure also that we can do our work that God requires of us, and we can let it alone: and therefore as sure as God's grace and help is necessary, so sure it is that we have that help that is necessary; for if we had not we could not be commanded to work, and there were no need of arguments or of reason, of deliberation or enquiry. . . . If in human actions, that is, actions of morality, there be a fate, then there is no contingency, and then all deliberation were the greatest folly in the world; because since only one part is possible, . . . the other part is but a chimaera, and therefore not subject to consultation. Add to this, if all our actions were predetermined, then one man were not better than another. . . . Princes may as well hang a true man as a thief, because this man no more breaks his law than the other, for neither of them do obey or disobey; but it is fortune that is hanged, and fortune that is advanced, and there is no such thing as virtue, no praise, and no law. . . . But certainly that is a strange proposition which affirms that nothing is possible but what is done. . . . If a man hath not a power to will or nill, it is to no purpose to write cases of conscience, or indeed to do anything as wise men should. A fool and a wise man differ not, a lazy man and a diligent, a good man and a bad, save only one hath a better star; they differ as a strong man and a weak: but though one be the better thing, he is not the better man. . . .

Whereas all men granting liberty of will in actions of natural life and common entercourse, many of them deny it in moral actions, and many more deny it in actions spiritual; they consider not that they evacuate and destroy the very nature and purpose of liberty and choice. . . . For the only end of liberty is to make us capable of laws, of virtue and reward, and to distinguish us from beasts by a distinct manner of approach to God. . . .

Liberty of choice in moral actions, that is, in all that can be good or bad, is agreeable to the whole method and purpose, the economy [system of regulations] and design of human nature and being. For we are a creature between angel and beast, and we understand something, and are ignorant of much, and the things that are before us are mixed of good and evil, and our duty hath much good and some evil, and sin hath some good and much evil, and therefore these things are and they are not to be pursued. There is a weight on both sides, and our propositions are probable, not true and false, but for several reasons seeming both to several persons. Now if to all this there were not a faculty that should proportionately, and in even measures, and by a symbolical progression, tend to these things, we could not understand, we could not see; we could not admire the numbers and music and proportions of the divine wisdom in our creation in relation to this order of things. For since in our objects there is good and evil in confusion or imperfect mixture, if our faculties tending to these objects were natural, and not deliberative and elective, they must take all in, or thrust all out, and either they must receive no good or admit every evil. . . . Difficulty makes virtue, and the contrariety of objects makes difficulty, and the various ends and amabilities [purposes and lovablenesses] make the contrariety, and liberty is the hand and fingers of the soul by which she picks and chooses, and if she gathers flowers she makes herself a garland of immortality. . . .

Liberty of will is like the motion of a magnetic needle toward the north, full of trembling and uncertainty till it be fixed in the beloved point: it wavers as long as it is free, and is at rest when it can choose no more. . . .

When the material actions are the same, there is nothing can distinguish the men that do them, but something within that can do this, or let it alone. Now because a good understanding, and a good fancy, and a great reason, and a great resolution, and a strong heart, and a healthful body, may be in a reprobate or vicious person, but a good will and the choice of virtue is only in a good man, it follows that all morality depends on the action of the will; and therefore that all other faculties are natural and necessary and obedient, this only is the empress, and is free, and mistress of the action. . . .

Ignorance is a sin when it is voluntary. The wicked say unto God, "We will not understand Thy ways." So the Psalmist complains, "He refused understanding." Now since in all the faculties the will of man hath a dominion, and is the cause of all moral actions, from thence they have their estimate, and are acquitted or condemned accordingly, . . . nothing makes fuel for the flames of hell but the will of man, and evil actions that are voluntary and chosen.

To will and to choose good is so necessary, and if we can, to do it is so required of us, that the very avoiding evil is exacted in that manner, that unless it be a doing good, it is a doing nothing at all, it is good for nothing, it will go for nothing. To eschew evil is a labour and a mighty work, it is a running from temptation, a shutting the doors against it, a praying against it, it is a flying from it when we can, and a resisting of it when we cannot. . . . The poor shepherd shall never be thanked for not contending for the archbishopric of Toledo, or not fighting against his prince, when nothing enters into his armoury but his bottle and his hook, and nothing into his head but that his sheep may wander in wholesome and pleasant pastures, and his lambs be free from dogs and foxes. A mere negative does nothing in God's service. The avoiding evil is neither good nor bad, unless it be by a positive act, unless the will be in it: and indeed as things are ordered it is many times harder to decline evil than to do good. *Ductor (Bk. iv, ch. i); X, 548-57.*

While one does not know how original sin can be derived, and another, who thinks he can, names a wrong way, and both the ways infer it to be another kind of thing than all the schools of learning teach—does it not too clearly demonstrate that all that infinite variety of fancies, agreeing in nothing but in an endless uncertainty, is nothing else but a being busy about the quiddities of a dream and the constituent parts of a shadow? *W.; VII, 543.*

Is hell so easy a pain or are the souls of children of so cheap, so contemptible a price, that God should so easily throw them into hell? God's goodness, which pardons many sins which we could avoid, will not so easily throw them into hell for what they could not avoid. God's goodness is against this. *Unum (ch. vi); VII, 253.*

It is a strange consideration to suppose an eternal torment to those to whom it was never threatened, to those who never heard of Christ, to those that lived probably well, to heathens of good lives . . . and that all this should be inflicted by God, who infinitely loves His creatures, who died for them, who pardons easily, and pities readily. It is certain that God's mercies are infinite, and it is also certain that the matter of eternal torments cannot truly be understood. And when the Schoolmen go about to reconcile the divine justice to that severity, and consider why God punishes eternally a temporal sin or a state of evil, and excuses much, and delights in our being saved, and would not have us die, and takes little things in exchange for great, they speak variously, and uncertainly, and unsatisfyingly. *S.W. (iii); IV, 43 f.*

In every one that was born, there are great inclinations to some good. *D.J.; VII, 505.*

To deny to the will of man powers of choice and election or the use of it in the actions of our life, destroys the immortality of the soul. . . . We may as well suppose an understanding that can never understand, and passions that can never desire or refuse, and a memory that can never remember, as a will that cannot choose. . . .

Unum (ch. vi); VII, 280.

Not God but ourselves are authors of our eternal deaths in case we do perish. *Unum (ch. vii); VII, 309.*

Sin creeps upon us in our education so tacitly and undiscernibly that we mistake the cause of it; and yet so prevalently and effectually that we judge it to be our very nature, and charge it upon Adam to lessen the imputation upon us or to increase the license or the confidence, when every one of us is the Adam, the "man of sin," and the parent of our own impurities. . . . Our proclivity to sin is occasioned by the accident and is caused by ourselves; whatever mischief Adam did to us, we do more to ourselves. *G.E. (Pt. i, § v); II, 103.*

For if God decrees us to be born sinners, then He makes us to be sinners; and then where is His goodness?

If God does damn any for that, He damns us for what we could not help, and for what Himself did; and then where is His justice?

If God sentences us to that damnation which He cannot in justice inflict, where is His wisdom?

If God for the sin of Adam brings upon us a necessity of sinning, where is our liberty? Where is our nature? What is become of all laws, and of all virtue and vice? How can men be distinguished from beasts, or the virtuous from the vicious?

If by the fall of Adam we are so wholly ruined in our faculties that we cannot do any good, but must do evil, how shall any man take care of his ways? or how can it be supposed he should strive against all vice, when he can excuse so much upon his nature? or indeed how shall he strive at all? For if all actual sins are derived from the original, and which is unavoidable, and yet an unresistible cause, then no man can take care to avoid any actual sin whose cause is natural and not to be declined; and then where is His providence and government?

If God does cast infants into hell for the sin of others, and yet did not condemn devils but for their own sin, where is His love to mankind?

If God chooseth the death of so many millions of persons who are no sinners upon their own stock, and yet swears that He does not love the death of a sinner, viz., sinning with his own choice: how can that [it] be credible He should love to kill innocents, and yet should love to spare the criminal? Where then is His mercy, and where is His truth?

D.J.; VII, 521.

ENDS AND MEANS

I have lived to see religion painted upon banners and thrust out of churches, and the temple turned into a tabernacle and that tabernacle made ambulatory, and covered with skins of beasts and torn curtains; and God to be worshipped, not as He is, the Father of our Lord Jesus, an afflicted Prince, the King of sufferings, nor as the God of peace. . . . But He is owned now rather as the Lord of hosts, which title He was pleased to lay aside when the kingdom of the gospel was preached by the Prince of peace. But when religion puts on armour and God is not acknowledged by His New Testament titles, religion may have in it the power of the sword, but not the power of godliness. . . .

And now the case is so with us that we are reduced to that religion which no man can forbid, which we can keep in the midst of a persecution by which the martyrs in the days of our fathers went to heaven; that by which we can be servants of God and receive the spirit of Christ, and make use of His comforts and live in His love and in charity with all men: and they that do so, cannot perish. *H.L.D.; III, 1, 3.*

Our quarrels and impertinent wranglings about religion are nothing else but the want of the measures of this state [of charity]. Our light is like a candle; every wind of vain doctrine blows it out or spends the wax and makes the light tremulous; but the lights of heaven are fixed and bright, and shine forever. *Un. D.; VIII, 381.*

In the scrutinies for righteousness and judgment, when it is enquired whether such a person be a good man or no, the meaning is not what does he believe, or what does he hope, but what he loves.

H.L. (ch. iv); III, 157.

No man can with all the wealth in the world buy so much skill as to be a good lutenist; he must go the same way that poor people do, he must learn and take pains. *H.L. (ch. iv); III, 202.*

"Many shall seek." The five foolish virgins sought; and they who shall tell Christ that they did miracles in His name, they sought; and the Pharisees sought; but all seeking, you see, shall not find. Some seek themselves alone, and they shall never find anything to satisfy them.

S.G.H.; I, 124.

The good example of the preacher is always the most prevailing homily; his life is his best sermon. *G.E.* (*Pt. i,* § *viii*)*; II, 165.*

War undoes us, and makes us violent; peace undoes us, and makes us wanton; prosperity makes us proud, adversity renders us impatient; plenty dissolves us and makes us tyrants; want makes us greedy, liars, and rapacious. *S.S.* (*viii*)*; IV, 425 f.*

If any private person in the simplicity and purity of his soul desires to find out a truth of which he is in search and inquisition, if he prays for wisdom we have a promise he shall be heard and answered. . . .

All that come to the knowledge of the truth must come to it by such means which are spiritual and holy dispositions, in order to a holy and spiritual end. *L.P.; V, 443 ff.*

There is one note amongst the rest, holiness of doctrine . . . and when we have found out all true doctrine . . . then we are bound to follow because we judge it true, not because the church hath said it; and this is to judge of the church by her doctrine, not of the doctrine by the church. *L.P.; V, 493.*

I will be of the man's religion if it be good, though he be not; but I will not make him my confessor. If he be not wise for himself, I will not sit down at his feet. *S.S.* (*xxii*)*; IV, 607.*

Anger should unyoke, and go to bed with the sun, since justice and authority laid by the rods and axes as soon as the sun unteamed his chariot. Plutarch reports that the Pythagoreans were strict observers of the very letter of this caution; for if anger had boiled up to the height of injury or reproach, before sunset they would shake hands, salute each other, and depart friends; for they were ashamed that the same anger which had disturbed the counsels of the day, should also trouble the quiet and dreams of the night, lest anger, by mingling with their rest and nightly fancies, should grow natural and habitual. Well, anger must last no longer; but neither may a Christian's anger last so long, for if his anger last a whole day, it will certainly, before night, sour into a crime. *G.E.* (*Pt. ii,* § *xii*)*; II, 436.*

When a storm of a sad mischance beats upon our spirits, turn it into some advantage by observing where it can serve another end, either of religion or prudence, of more safety or less envy: it will turn into something that is good, if we list to make it so; at least it may make us weary of the world's vanity and take off our confidence from uncertain riches, and make our spirits to dwell in those regions where content dwells essentially. If it does any good to our souls, it hath made more than sufficient recompense for all the temporal affliction. He that threw a stone at a dog and hit his cruel step-mother, said that although he intended it otherwise, yet the stone was not quite lost: and if we fail in the first design, if we bring it home to another equally to content us, or more to profit us, then we have put our conditions past the power of chance.

H.L. (ch. ii); III, 88.

That which we are taught by the holy Spirit of God, this new nature, this vital principle within us, it is that which is worth our learning; not vain and empty, idle and insignificant notions, in which when you have laboured till your eyes are fixed in their orbs and your flesh unfixed from its bones, you are no better and no wiser. . . . What are you the better if any man should pretend to teach you whether every angel makes a species, and what is the individuation of the soul in the state of separation? what are you the wiser if you should study and find out what place Adam should forever have lived in if he had not fallen? and what is any man the more learned if he hears the disputes whether Adam should have multiplied children in the state of innocence? and what would have been the event of things if one child had been born before his father's sin?

Too many scholars have lived upon air and empty notions for many ages past, and troubled themselves with tying and untying knots, like hypochondriacs in a fit of melancholy, thinking of nothing and troubling themselves with nothing and falling out about nothings, and being very wise and very learned in things that are not and work not, and were never planted in Paradise by the finger of God. *Un. D.; VIII, 383 f.*

The lazy man is not only unprofitable, but also accursed, and he groans under the load of his time, which yet passes over the active man light as a dream, or the feathers of a bird; while the disemployed is a disease and like a long sleepless night to himself, and a load unto his country. *S.S. (xxv); IV, 641.*

The truth may lose much of its reputation by its mixture with error, and the error may become more plausible by reason of its conjunction with truth. And this we see by too much experience, for we see many truths are blasted in their reputation because persons whom we think we hate upon just grounds of religion have taught them. And it was plain enough in the case of Maldonat, that said of an explication of a place of scripture that it was most agreeable to antiquity, but because Calvin had so expounded it, he therefore chose a new one. *L.P.; V, 502.*

We must take care that the end of our actions be all of gold. If they be designed well they are likely to end well . . . for in the service of God a golden head shall never have the feet of clay.

Ductor (*Bk. iv, ch. ii*)*; X, 659.*

Concerning myself I shall make no request to my reader but that he will charitably believe I mean well, and have done my best. If any man be troubled that he hath expected this nothing so long, I cannot make him other answer but that I am afraid it is now too soon; and I bless God that I had abilities of health and leisure now at last to finish it: . . . which if I have improved to God's glory, or to the comfort and institution of any one, He and I both have our ends, and God will have His glory; and that's a good conclusion, and to that I humbly dedicate my book.

From my study in Portmore in Kilultagh, October 5, 1659.

Ductor (*Bk. i, pref.*)*; IX, xxiii.*

THE FLESH AND THE SPIRIT

God is especially present in the hearts of His people, by His Holy Spirit: and indeed the hearts of holy men are temples in the truth of things, and in type and shadow they are heaven itself. For God reigns in the hearts of His servants: there is His kingdom. . . . God dwells in our hearts by faith, and Christ by His spirit, and the Spirit by His purities: so that we are also cabinets of the mysterious Trinity. And what is this short of heaven itself, but as infancy is short of manhood, and letters of words? The same state of life it is, but not the same age. It is heaven in a looking-glass, dark but yet true, representing the beauties of the soul and the graces of God and the images of His eternal glory, by the reality of a special presence. . . .

God is in every creature: be cruel towards none, neither abuse any by intemperance. Remember that the creatures and every member of thy own body, is one of the lesser cabinets and receptacles of God. . . .

We are of the same household with God. . . .

Let no riches make me ever forget myself, no poverty ever make me to forget Thee.

H.L. (*ch. i*)*; III, 24, 27 f., 38.*

Now because a man cannot serve two masters; because he cannot vigorously attend two objects; because there can be but one living soul in any living creature: if the world have got possession, talk no more of your questions, shut your bibles, and read no more of the words of God to them, for they cannot "tell of the doctrine whether it be of God," or of the world. *Un. D.; VIII, 373.*

The Germans use to mingle music with their bowls, and drink by the measure of the six notes of music:

Ut re*levet* mi*serum* fa*tum* so*litosque* la*bores.* But they sing so long that they forget not their sorrow only but their virtue also and their religion. And there are some men that fall into drunkenness because they would forget a lighter calamity, running into the fire to cure a calenture and beating their brains out to be quit of the aching of their heads. . . .

Even when a man hath no necessity upon him, no pungent sorrow, or natural or artificial necessity, it is lawful in some cases of eating and drinking to receive pleasure and intend it. . . .

It is lawful when a man needs meat to choose the pleasanter. . . . This is as lawful as to smell of a rose, or to lie in feathers, or change the posture of our body in bed for ease; or to hear music, or to walk in gardens rather than the highways. And God hath given us leave to be delighted in those things which He made to that purpose that we may also be delighted in Him that gives them. . . .

Let the pleasure as it came with meat, so also pass away with it. Philoxenus was a beast: "he wished his throat as long as a crane's," that he might be long in swallowing his pleasant morsels; "he mourned because the pleasure of eating was not spread over all his body," that he might have been an epicure in his hands. And indeed if we consider it rightly, great eating and drinking is not the greatest pleasure of the taste but of the touch; and Philoxenus might feel the unctious juice slide softly down his throat, but he could not taste it in the middle of the long neck; and we see that they who mean to feast exactly or delight the palate . . . take up little proportions and spread them upon the tongue or palate, but full morsels and great draughts are easy and soft to the touch. But so is the feeling of silk, or handling of a melon, or a mole's skin—and as delicious, too, as eating when it goes beyond the appetites of nature and the proper pleasures of taste, which cannot be perceived but by a temperate man. And therefore let not the pleasure be intended beyond the taste. . . . Do not run to it beforehand, nor chew the cud when the meal is done. *S.W. (xvi); IV, 201 ff.*

Pittacus was a wise and valiant man, but his wife overthrew the table when he had invited his friends; upon which the good man, to excuse her incivility and his own misfortune, said that "every man had one evil, and he was most happy that had but that alone."

H.L. (ch. ii); III, 98.

The greatest vanity of this world is remarkable in this, that all its joys summed up together are not big enough to counterpoise the evil of one sharp disease, or to allay a sorrow. For imagine a man great in his dominion as Cyrus, rich as Solomon, victorious as David, beloved like Titus, learned as Trismegist, powerful as all the Roman greatness: all this and the results of all this give him no more pleasure in the midst of a fever or the tortures of the stone, than if he were only lord of a little dish, and a dish-full of fountain water. *S.S. (xviii); IV, 551.*

[Sin] pleases the senses, but diseases the spirit, and wounds. . . . It is gravel in the teeth. *S.W. (xix); IV, 240.*

It was not without mystery observed among the ancients that they who made gods of gold and silver, of hope and fear, peace and fortune, garlic and onions, beasts and serpents, and a quartan ague,* yet never deified money: meaning that however wealth was admired by common or abused understandings, yet from riches . . . no moment could be added to a man's real content or happiness. *H.L. (ch. ii); III, 102.*

To desire more than our life needs is to desire abundance, and that is covetousness, and that is the root of all evil. . . . There were no wars in those days when men did drink in a treen [wooden] cup. *Unum; VII, 126.*

Our excellent bodies and useful faculties, the upright motion and the tenacious hand, the fair appetites and proportioned satisfactions, our speech and our perceptions, our acts of life, the rare invention of letters, and the use of writing and speaking at distance, the intervals of rest and labour (either of which if they were perpetual would be intolerable), the needs of nature and the provisions of providence, sleep and business, refreshments of the body and entertainments of the soul: these are to be reckoned as acts of bounty rather than mercy; God gave us these when He made us. *S.S. (xxv); IV, 635.*

The dispersed excellencies and blessings of many men if given to one, would not make a handsome but a monstrous fortune. . . . Let Euphorion sleep quietly with his old rich wife, and let Medius drink on with Alexander; and remember thou canst not have the riches of the first unless you have the old wife too, nor the favor which the second had with his prince unless you buy it at his price. *H.L. (ch. ii); III, 97.*

You move them [fornicators] no more than if you should read one of Tully's orations to a mule, for the truth is they have no power to resist it, much less to master it. . . . And yet their heart deceives them,

* Occurring every fourth day.

not because it cannot resist the temptation but because it will not go about it: for it is certain, the heart can if it list. *S.S. (vii); IV, 412.*

Nothing rules a man in private but God and his own desires; and they give laws in a wilderness and accuse in a cloister.
G.E. (Pt. i, § v); II, 120.

Certain it is that the body does hinder many actions of the soul: it is an imperfect body and a diseased brain, or a violent passion, that makes fools. No man hath a foolish soul. *F.C.C.; VIII, 439.*

There is so near a conjunction between soul and body that it is no wonder if God, meaning to glorify both by the means of a spiritual life, suffers spirit and matter to communicate in effects and mutual impresses. . . . Since the body hath all its life from its conjunction with the soul, why not also the perfection of life, according to its present capacity (that is, health and duration) from the perfection of the soul? . . .

But this problem in christian philosophy is yet more intelligible and will be reduced to certain experience, if we consider good life in union and concretion with particular, material, and circumstantiate actions of piety: for these have great powers and influences, even in nature, to restore health and preserve our lives. Witness the sweet sleeps of temperate persons and their constant appetite; which Timotheus the son of Conon observed, when he dieted in Plato's academy with severe and moderated diet, "they that sup with Plato are well the next day."
G.E. (Pt. iii, § xiii); II, 532 f.

Jesus . . . tells them He was Jesus of Nazareth whom they sought. But this also, which was an answer so gentle, had in it a strength greater than the eastern wind or the voice of thunder; for God was in that "still voice" and it struck them down to the ground. . . . In this instance there was a rare mixture of effects, as there was in Christ, of natures: the voice of a man, and the power of God. . . . The divinity and humanity did so communicate in effects that no great action passed but it was like the sun shining through a cloud, or a beauty with a thin veil drawn over it. *G.E. (Pt. iii, § xv); II, 665 f.*

If he [a man] be willing, what hinders him to love, to pardon, to wish well, to desire? The willing is the doing in this case; and he that says he is willing to do his duty but he cannot, does not understand what he says. For all the duty of the inner man consists in the actions of the will, and there they are seated, and to it all the inferior faculties obey in those things which are direct emanations and effects of will. He that desires to love God, does love Him. . . .

If the spirit and the heart be willing, it will pass on to outward actions in all things. . . . For these things which are in our hand are under the power of the will, and therefore are to be commanded by it. He that says to the naked, "Be warm and clothed," and gives him not the garment that lies by him or money to buy one, mocks God and the poor and himself. *S.W. (xi); IV, 141.*

The body must bow when the soul worships, and the hand must help when the soul pities, and both together do the work of a holy religion. The body alone can never serve God without the conjunction and preceding act of the soul, and sometimes the soul without the body is imperfect and vain. *S.W. (xii); IV, 148.*

Sickness is the more tolerable because it cures very many evils and takes away the sense of all the cross fortunes which amaze the spirits of some men, and transport them certainly beyond all the limits of patience. Here all losses and disgraces, domestic cares and public evils, the apprehensions of pity and a sociable calamity, the fears of want and the troubles of ambition, lie down and rest upon the sick man's pillow. . . .

And yet after all this, sickness leaves in us appetites so strong, and apprehensions so sensible and delights so many, and good things in so great a degree, that a healthless body and a sad disease do seldom make men weary of this world, but still they would fain find an excuse to live. *H.D. (ch. iii); III, 316 f.*

As temperance begins to go away . . . every new goblet is still less delicious, and cannot be endured but as men force nature by violence to stay longer than she would. . . . And when they cannot escape, they pour it in and receive it with as much pleasure as the old women have in the Lapland dances. They dance the round, but there is a horror and a harshness in the music; and they call it pleasure because men bid them do so, but there is a devil in the company. *S.W. (xix); IV, 237.*

By the use of the tongue God hath distinguished us from beasts, and by the well or ill using it we are distinguished from one another; and therefore though silence be innocent as death, harmless as a rose's breath to a distant passenger, yet it is rather the state of death than life; and therefore when the Egyptians sacrificed to Harpocrates, their god of silence, in the midst of their rites they cried out, "the tongue is an angel"; good or bad, that's as it happens. Silence was to them a god, but the tongue is greater: it is the band of human intercourse and makes men apt to unite in societies and republics. . . . But the tongue is a fountain both of bitter waters and of pleasant; it sends forth blessing and cursing; it praises God and rails at men; it is sometimes set on fire, and then it puts whole cities in combustion; it is unruly, and no more to be restrained than the breath of a tempest; it is volatile and fugitive; reason should go before it, and when it does not, repentance comes after it; it was intended for an organ of the divine praises, but the devil often plays upon it, and then it sounds like the screech-owl or the groans of death: sorrow and shame, folly and repentance, are the notes and formidable accents of that discord. *S.W. (xxii); IV, 274 f.*

Though that which is compounded of elements returns to its material and corruptible principles, yet the soul, which is a "particle of the divine breath,"* returns to its own divine original, where there is no death or dissolution. *F.G.D.; VIII, 545.*

Some laws fit our natures as they are common to us and beasts, some fit us as we are next to angels, and some fit us as we are designed to immortality and the fruition of God; and the laws of nature do grow as our natures do. *Ductor (Bk. ii, ch.ii); IX, 409.*

If a man believes learning to be the only or chiefest ornament and beauty of souls, that which will enoble him to a fair employment in his own time, and an honourable memory to succeeding ages: this if he believes heartily, it hath power to make him endure catarrhs, gouts, hypochondriacal passions, to read until his eyes almost fix in their orbs, to despise the pleasures of idleness or tedious sports, and to undervalue whatsoever does not co-operate to the end of his faith, the desire of learning.
G.E. (Pt. ii, § x); II, 303.

Be severe in your judgment concerning your proportions, and let no occasion make you enlarge far beyond your ordinary. For a man is surprised by parts; and while he thinks one glass more will not make him drunk, that one glass hath disabled him from well discerning his present condition and neighbour danger. . . . But remember this, whenever you begin to consider whether you may safely take one draught more, it is then high time to give over: let that be accounted a sign late enough to break off, for every reason to doubt is a sufficient reason to part the company. *H.L. (ch. ii); III, 53.*

He that feasts every day, feasts no day; and however you treat yourselves, sometimes you will need to be refreshed beyond it; but what will you have for a festival if you wear crowns every day?
S.W. (xvi); IV, 193

He that is proud of riches is a fool. For if he be exalted above his neighbours because he hath more gold, how much inferior is he to a gold mine? how much is he to give place to a chain of pearl [*sic*], or a knot of diamonds? *H.L. (ch. ii); III, 69.*

* Horace, *Satires*, lib. ii, 2*nd* satire.

There is no wise or good man that would change persons or conditions entirely with any man in the world. It may be he would have one man's wealth added to himself, or the power of a second, or the learning of a third; but still he would receive these into his own person, because he loves that best and therefore esteems it best, and therefore overvalues all that which he is before all that which any other man in the world can be. . . . For every man hath desires of his own and objects just fitted to them without which he cannot be, unless he were not himself. And let every man that loves himself so well as to love himself before all the world, consider if he have not something for which in the whole he values far more than he can value any man else. There is therefore no reason to take the finest feathers from all the winged nation to deck that bird that thinks already she is more valuable than any of the inhabitants of the air. Either change all or none; cease to love yourself best, or be content with that portion of being and blessing for which you love yourself so well. *H.L. (ch. ii); III, 89.*

Strange . . . it is that for the stomach, which is scarce a span long, there should be provided so many furnaces and ovens, huge fires and an army of cooks, cellars swimming with wine and granaries sweating with corn; and that into one belly should enter the vintage of many nations, the spoils of distant provinces and the shell-fishes of several seas. When the heathens feasted their gods, they gave nothing but a fat ox, a ram, or a kid; they poured a little wine upon the altar and burned a handful of gum: but when they feasted themselves, they had many vessels filled with Campanian wine, turtles of Liguria, Sicilian beeves, and wheat from Egypt, wild boars from Illyrium, and Grecian sheep; variety and load and cost and curiosity: and so do we. It is so little we spend in religion and so very much upon ourselves, so little to the poor and so without measure to make ourselves sick. *S.W. (xv); IV, 191.*

I am fallen into the hands of publicans and sequestrators, and they have taken all from me: what now? let me look about me. They have left me the sun and moon, fire and water, a loving wife, and many friends to pity me and some to relieve me, and I can still discourse. And unless I list they have not taken away my merry countenance and my cheerful spirit and a good conscience: they still have left me the providence of God, and all the promises of the gospel, and my religion, and my hopes of heaven, and my charity to them, too; and still I sleep and digest, I eat and drink, I read and meditate; I can walk in my neighbour's pleasant fields, and see the varieties of natural beauties, and delight in all that in which God delights: that is, in virtue and wisdom, in the whole creation, and in God himself. And he that hath so many causes of joy and so great, is very much in love with sorrow and peevishness, who loses all these pleasures and chooses to sit down upon his little handful of thorns. *H.L. (ch. ii); III, 91.*

THE MIND, THE SOUL

The ancients, especially the scholars of Epicurus, believed that no [wicked] man could be secured or quiet in his spirit from being discovered; "they are not secure, even when they are safe." . . . Every whisper is concerning them and all new noises are arrests to their spirits; and the day is too light and the night is too horrid, and both are the most opportune for their discovery. . . . Many secret crimes have been published by dreams and talkings in their sleep . . . and what their understanding kept a guard upon, their fancy let loose; fear was the bars and locks but sleep became the key to open, even then when all the senses were shut and God ruled alone without the choice and discourse of man. And though no man regards the wilder talkings of a distracted man, yet it hath sometimes happened that a delirium and a fever, fear of death and the intolerable apprehensions of damnation, have opened the cabinet of sin and brought to light all that was acted in the curtains of night. . . . Many persons have betrayed themselves by their own fears, and knowing themselves never to be secure enough have gone to purge themselves of what nobody suspected them; offered an apology when they had no accuser but one within, which, like a thorn in the flesh or like "a word in a fool's heart" was uneasy till it came out. When men are over busy in justifying themselves, it is a sign themselves think they need it. . . . Murder and treason have by such strange ways been revealed as if God had appointed an angel president of the revelation. . . . Mistaking names, false inscriptions, errors of messengers, faction of the parties, fear in the actors, horror in the action, the majesty of the person, the restlessness of the mind, distracted looks, weariness of the spirit . . . make the covers of the most secret sin transparent as a net, and visible as the Chian wines in the purest crystal. *S.W. (xxi); IV, 264 f.*

All quarrellings and contentions at law for little matters are arguments of impatience, of a peevish spirit, and an uncharitable mind. He is a very miserable man that is unquiet when a mouse runs over his shoe, or a fly does kiss his cheek. *Wor. Com. (ch. iv); VIII, 143.*

Notices of things terrible and true pass through his [the wicked man's] understanding as an eagle through the air; as long as her flight lasted the air was shaken, but there remains no path behind her.

Un. D.; VIII, 376 f.

The wife that lies by his side knows not at what the guilty man looks pale, but something that is within the bosom knows; and no pompousness of condition can secure the man, and no witty cruelty can equal the torment. . . .

An evil conscience makes man a coward, timorous as a child in a church porch at midnight. . . .

God oftentimes awakens a man by a sudden dash of thunder and lightning, and makes the conscience sick and troublesome . . . and sometimes every dream, or sad story that the man hath heard, the flying of birds, and the hissing of serpents, or the fall of waters, or the beating of a watch, or the noise of a cricket, or a superstitious tale, is suffered to do the man a mischief and to increase his fear.

Ductor (Bk. i, ch. i); IX, 20, 25, 28.

A man committing a foul sin . . . perceives all the world hates him for his crime. . . .

It cannot be denied but opinion also hath some hand in this affair; and some men are affrighted from their cradle in some instances . . . and the fears of childhood are not shaken from the conscience in old age: as we see the persuasions of childhood in moral actions are permanent. . . . Education and society and country customs, and states of life, and the religion or sect of the man's professing, hath influence into their portions of this effect. *Ductor (Bk. i, ch. i); IX, 30 f.*

A man's heart is infinitely deceitful, unknown to itself, not certain in his own acts, praying one way and desiring another, wandering and imperfect, loose and various, worshipping God and entertaining sin, following what it hates and running from what it flatters, loving to be tempted and betrayed. *H.D. (ch. v); III, 434.*

Living and waking men have one world in common; they use the same air and fire, and discourse by the same principles of logic and reason: but men that are asleep have every one a world to himself.

S.W. (ix); IV, 113.

The crowing of a cock, the singing of a lark, the dawning of the day, and the washing their hands, are to them [those who know "the secret of the spirit"] competent memorials of religion. *Un. D.; VIII, 377.*

When we see a child strike a servant rudely or jeer a silly person, or wittily cheat his play-fellow, or talk words light as the skirt of a summer garment, we laugh and are delighted with the wit and confidence of the boy, and encourage such hopeful beginnings. And in the meantime we consider not that from these beginnings he shall grow up till he become a tyrant, an oppressor, a goat, and a traitor. . . . "No man is discerned to be vicious so soon as he is so"; and vices have their infancy and their childhood; and it cannot be expected that in a child's age should be the vice of a man; that were monstrous, as if he wore a beard in his cradle. "And we do not believe that a serpent's sting does just then grow, when he strikes us in a vital part"; the venom and the little spear was there when it first began to creep from his little shell. And little boldnesses and looser words, and wranglings for nuts and lying for trifles, are of the same proportion to the malice of a child as impudence and duels and injurious law-suits, and false witness in judgment, and perjuries, are in men. *S.S. (xvi); IV, 526.*

Education is so great and so invincible a prejudice [pre-judgment] that he who masters the inconvenience of it is more to be commended than he can justly be blamed that complies with it. For men do not always call them principles which are the prime fountains of reason . . . but they are principles which they are first taught, which they sucked in next to their milk. . . . Whatsoever is taught to them at first they believe infinitely, for they know nothing to the contrary; they have had no other masters whose theorems might abate the strength of their first persuasions . . . and this is helped forward very much by the advantage of love and veneration which we have to the first parents of our persuasions. . . . And it is strange that all the Dominicans should be of one opinion in the matter of predetermination and immaculate conception, and all the Franciscans of the quite contrary, as if their understandings were formed in a different mould and furnished with various principles by their very rule. *L.P.; V, 503 f.*

[Conscience] ever speaks loudest when the man is poor, or sick, or miserable. . . . Then the calamity swells and conscience increases the trouble. . . . Then every bush is a wild beast, and every shadow is a ghost, and every glow-worm is a dead man's candle, every lantern is a spirit. *Ductor (Bk. i, ch. i); IX, 22 f.*

A scruple is a great trouble of mind proceeding from a little motive and a great indisposition, by which the conscience, though sufficiently determined by proper arguments, dares not proceed to action, or if it do, it cannot rest.

Said Solomon, "too violent blowing draws blood from the nose"; that is, an enquiry after determination, and searching into little corners, and measuring actions by atoms, and unnatural measures, and being over righteous, is the way not to govern, but to disorder our conscience.

That it is a great trouble, is a daily experiment and a sad sight: some persons dare not eat for fear of gluttony, they fear that they shall sleep too much, and that keeps them waking and troubles their heads more, and then their scruples increase. . . .

Scruple is a little stone in the foot, if you set it upon the ground it hurts you, if you hold it up you cannot go forward; it is a trouble where the trouble is over, a doubt when doubts are resolved; it is a little party behind a hedge when the main army is broken and the field cleared; and when the conscience is instructed in its way and girt for action, a light trifling reason or an absurd fear hinders it from beginning the journey, or proceeding in the way, or resting at the journey's end.

Very often it hath no reason at all for its inducement, but proceeds from indisposition of body, pusillanimity, melancholy, a troubled head, sleepless nights, the society of the timorous; from solitariness, ignorance, or unseasoned [and] imprudent notices of things, indigested learning, strong fancy and weak judgment; from anything that may abuse the reason into irresolution and restlessness. It is indeed a direct walking in the dark, where we see nothing to affright us, but we fancy many things, and the phantasms produced in the lower regions of fancy, and nursed by folly, and borne upon the arms of fear do trouble us.

But if reason be its parent, then it is born in the twilight, and the mother is so little that the daughter is a fly with a short head and a long sting, enough to trouble a wise man, but not enough to satisfy the appetite of a little bird. The reason of a scruple is ever as obscure as the light of a glow-worm, not fit to govern any action, and yet is suffered to stand in the midst of all its enemies, and like the flies of Egypt vex and trouble the whole army. *Ductor (Bk. i, ch. vi); IX, 262 ff.*

Against a doubting conscience a man may not work, but against a scrupulous he may. For a scrupulous conscience does not take away the proper determination of the understanding; but it is like a woman handling of a frog or a chicken, which all their friends tell them can do them no hurt, and they are convinced in reason that they cannot, they believe it and know it, and yet when they take the little creature into their hands they shriek, and sometimes hold fast and find their fears confuted, and sometimes they let go, and find their reason useless.

Ductor (Bk. i, ch. vi); IX, 266.

The soul is all that whereby we may be, and without which we cannot be, happy. It is not the eye that sees the beauties of the heaven, nor the ear that hears the sweetnesses of music, or the glad tidings of a prosperous accident, but the soul that perceives all the relishes of sensual and intellectual perfections. And the more noble and excellent the soul is, the greater and more savoury are its perceptions. And if a child beholds the rich ermine, or the diamonds of a starry night, or the order of the world, or hears the discourses of an apostle—because he makes no reflex acts upon himself, and sees not that he sees, he can have but the pleasure of a fool or the deliciousness of a mule. *S.S. (xix); IV, 560.*

The soul of man . . . reflects upon its own inferior actions of particular sense or general understanding; but because it knows little of its own nature, the manners of volition, the immediate instruments of understanding, the way how it comes to meditate; and cannot discern how a sudden thought arrives, or the solution of a doubt not depending upon preceding premises: therefore above half of its pleasures are abated and its own worth less understood. *S.S.* (*xix*)*; IV, 561.*

No man sins against his will directly. *S.S.* (*xvii*)*; IV, 542.*

We all profess that God is almighty, that all His promises are certain; and yet when it comes to a pinch, we find that man to be more confident that hath ten thousand pounds in his purse than he that reads God's promises over ten thousand times. *G.E.* (*Pt. ii, § x*)*; II, 304.*

If our passions and foolish principles would give us leave to understand it, the precise duty of forgiveness is a perfect negative: it is a letting things alone as they are, and making no more evils in the world, in which already there was one too many, even that which thou didst suffer. And indeed that forgiveness is the best which is the most perfect negative; that is, "in malice be children," whose petty quarrels though they be fierce as a sudden spark, yet they are as innocent as the softest part of their own flesh, and as soon out as that sudden spark and forgotten perfectly as their first dream: and that's true forgiveness.
Wor. Com. (*ch. iv*)*; VIII, 126.*

All the interval between our losing baptismal grace and the day of our death we walk in a cloud, having lost the certain knowledge of our present condition by our prevarications. And indeed it is a very hard thing for a man to know his own heart. *G.E.* (*Pt. iii, § xiii*)*; II, 550.*

It was soberly spoken of Tertullian, "our conscience is the best argument in the world to prove there is a God." For conscience is God's deputy, and the inferior must suppose a superior. . . . It is impossible that any man should be an atheist if he have any conscience; and for this reason it is there have been so few atheists in the world, because it is so hard for men to lose their conscience wholly. . . .

A man may as well cease to be a man as to be wholly without conscience. . . . This is a perpetual pulse, and though it may be interrupted, yet if the man be alive it will beat before he dies. . . .
Ductor (*Bk. i, ch. i*)*; IX, 4 ff.*

Said Plato, "Every soul loses truth very unwillingly." Every man is so great a lover of truth that if he hath it not he loves to believe he hath, and would fain have all the world to believe as he does: either presuming that he hath truth, or else hating to be deceived, or to be esteemed a cheated and an abused person. R. Moses [Maimonides?] said, "If a man be a Samaritan," that is, a hated person, a person from whom you differ in matter of religion, "yet steal not his mind away, but speak truth to him honestly and ingenuously." A man's soul loves to dwell in truth, it is his resting-place; and if you take him from thence, you take him into strange regions, a place of banishment and dishonor.

S.S. (xxiii); IV, 611 f.

Religion can turn into a snare. It may be abused into superstition, it may become weariness in the spirit and tempt to tediousness, to hatred, and despair; and many persons through their indiscreet conduct and furious marches, and great loads taken upon tender shoulders and unexperienced, have come to be perfect haters of their joy and despisers of all their hopes. *S.W. (xiv); IV, 176.*

They are fancies of a too confident opinion and over-valuing of ourselves, when we think the very being of a church is concerned in our mistakes. And if all the world be against us, we are not ashamed of our folly, but think truth is failed from among the children of men, and the church is at a loss and the current derived from the first emanations is dried up; and then he that is boldest to publish his follies is also as apt to mistake his own boldness for "a call from God," as he did at first his own vain opinion for a necessary truth. . . . He that thinks every shaking of the ark is absolute ruin to it, when peradventure it was but the weakness of his own eyes that made him fancy what was not, may also think he hears a call from above to support it, which indeed was nothing but a noise in his own head: and there is no cure for this, but to cure the man and set his head right.

D.I.O.M. (§ viii); I, 56.

It is unnatural and unreasonable to persecute disagreeing opinions. Unnatural: for understanding, being a thing wholly spiritual, cannot be restrained, and therefore neither punished by corporal afflictions. It is *in aliena republica,* a matter of another world. You may as well cure the colic by brushing a man's clothes, or fill a man's belly with a syllogism . . . .

Force in matters of opinion can do no good, but is very apt to do hurt; for no man can change his opinion when he will, or be satisfied in his reason that his opinion is false because discountenanced . . . . To use force may make him a hypocrite, but never to be a right believer.

L.P.; V, 522 f.

If a man throws away his gold, as did Crates the Theban or the proud philosopher Diogenes, and yet leaves a spirit high, airy, and fantastical, and vain, pleasing himself and with complacency reflecting upon his own act, his poverty is but a circumstance of pride, and the opportunity of an imaginery and a secular greatness.

G.E. (*Pt. ii,* § *xii*) *; II, 394.*

Every man understands by his affections more than by his reason: and when the wolf in the fable went to school to learn to spell, whatever letters were told him, he could never make anything of them but *agnus;* he thought of nothing but his belly . . . . A man's mind must be like your proposition before it can be entertained: for whatever you put into a man it will smell of the vessel: it is a man's mind that gives the emphasis and makes your argument to prevail. *Un. D.; VIII, 369.*

Truth enters into the heart of man when it is empty and clean and still; but when the mind is shaken with passion as with a storm, you can never "hear the voice of the charmer though he charm very wisely." [Psalm LVIII, 5] *Un.D.; VIII, 374.*

It is necessary that we begin speedily, lest we have no time to begin that work which ought in some measure to be finished before we die. He that is uncertain what to do shall never do anything well; and there is no infirmity greater than that a man shall not be able to determine himself what he ought to do. *Unum.* (*ch. viii*) *; VII, 384.*

There is a strange spring and secret principle in every man's understanding, that it is oftentimes turned about by such impulses of which no man can give an account. But we all remember a most wonderful instance of it, in the disputation between the two Reynold's, John and William; the former of which, being a Papist, and the later [*sic*] a Protestant, met and disputed with a purpose to confute and to convert each other; and so they did: for those arguments which were used prevailed fully against their adversary and yet did not prevail with themselves. The Papist turned Protestant and the Protestant became a Papist, and so remained to their dying day . . . .

[A tractable Protestant] deplores that many men study hard and understand little; that they dispute earnestly and understand not one another at all; that affections creep so certainly and mingle with their arguing that the argument is lost, and nothing remains but the conflict of two adversaries' affections; that a man is so willing, so easy, so ready to believe what makes for his opinion, so hard to understand an argument against himself, that it is plain it is the principle within, not the argument without, that determines him . . . . He considers there is such ambiguity in words, by which all lawgivers express their meaning; that there is such abstruseness in mysteries of religion that some things are so much too high for us that we cannot understand them rightly; . . . that there is such variety of human understandings that men's faces differ not so much as their souls; and that if there were not so much difficulty in things, yet they could not but be variously apprehended by several men; and then considering that in twenty opinions it may be not one of them is true . . . .

In all religions, in all societies, in all families, and in all things, opinions differ; and since opinions are too often begot by passion, by passions and violences they are kept; and every man is too apt to overvalue his own opinion . . . and as he loves those that think as he does, so he is ready to hate them that do not; and then secretly from wishing evil to him, he is apt to believe evil will come to him, and that it is just it should: and by this time the opinion is troublesome, and puts other men upon their guard against it; and then while passion reigns and reason is modest and patient and talks not loud like a storm, victory is more regarded than truth, and men call God into the party, and His judgments are used for arguments, and the threatenings of the scripture are snatched up in haste, and men throw "arrows, firebrands, and death," and by this time all the world is in an uproar.

D.P. (Pt. ii, Bk. i, § vii); VI, 476 ff.

Every sort of men hath some religion or other by the measures of which they proportion their lives and their prayers. . . . If he be a tyrant or a usurper, a robber or a murderer, he hath his Laverna [goddess of rogues and thieves], too, by which all his desires are guided and his prayers directed and his petitions furnished. *S.W. (v); IV, 59.*

We do not know our own bodies, not what is within us, nor what ails us when we are sick, nor whereof we are made; nay, we oftentimes cannot tell what we think, or believe, or love. We desire and hate the same thing, speak against and run after it . . . . We weigh deeper what is extrinsical to a question than what is in its nature; and oftener regard who speaks than what is said. *Unum (ch. vi); VII, 286.*

We see many times and in many instances that a great memory is hindered and put out, and we thirty years after come to think of some thing that lay so long under a curtain; we think of it suddenly, and without a line of deduction or proper consequence. . . . For even the memory of . . . the dullest person now alive, is so great, and by God made so sure a record of all that ever he did, that as soon as ever God shall but tune our instrument and draw the curtains, and but light up the candle of immortality, there we shall find it all, there we shall see all. *F.C.C.; VIII, 441 f.*

REASON AND THINGS REASONABLE*

Every man hath enough of knowledge to make him good if he please: and it is infinitely culpable and criminal that men by their industry shall become so wise in the affairs of the world, and so ignorant in that which is their eternal interest: it is because they love it not. No man looks for emeralds in a tree, nor cuts his vines hoping they will bleed rubies or weep pearls. Which of all the heathens or Christians ever went to take goats in the Tyrrhene waters, or looked for crystal in a furnace? Many know what pits have the best oysters, and where the fattest tortoise feeds. And yet they look for immortality in money, and dig deep into the earth, hoping there to find that blessedness their reason tells them dwells beyond the stars.

Ductor (Bk. iv, ch. i); X, 617.

Reason is such a box of quicksilver that it abides no where; it dwells in no settled mansion; it is like a dove's neck or a changeable taffeta; it looks to me otherwise than to you who do not stand in the same light that I do; and if we enquire after the law of nature by the rules of our reason, we shall be uncertain as the discourses of the people or the dreams of disturbed fancies. *Ductor (Bk. ii, ch. i); IX, 293.*

Now let us take a man that pretends he hath the "gift of prayer," and loves to pray *ex tempore;* I suppose his thoughts go a little before his tongue. I demand then whether cannot this man, when it is once come into his head, hold his tongue and write down what he hath conceived? If his first conceptions were of God and God's spirit, then they are so still even when they are written. Or is the Spirit departed from him upon the sight of a pen and inkhorn? *S.F.L.; V, 271 f.*

Whatsoever is against right reason, that no faith can oblige us to believe. . . .

If therefore any society of men calls upon us to believe in our religion what is false in our experience, to affirm that to be done which we know is impossible it ever can be done, to wink hard that we may see the better . . . they make religion so to be seated in the will that our understanding will be useless and can never minister to it. But as he that shuts the eye hard and with violence curls the eyelid, forces a fantastic fire from the crystalline humour, and espies a light that never shines, and sees thousands of little fires that never burn: so is he that

* In his treatment of reason Taylor stressed the spiritual element in man's judgment as well as the practical and the purely logical.

blinds the eye of his reason and pretends to see by an eye of faith. He makes little images of notion and some atoms dance before him, but he is not guided by the light nor instructed by the proposition, but sees like a man in his sleep. . . . He that speaks against his own reason speaks against his own conscience, and therefore it is certain no man serves God with a good conscience that serves Him against his reason.

Wor. Com. (*ch. iii*)*; VIII, 106.*

If any one of the people can prescribe or make it necessary to change the law, then everyone can; and by this time every new opinion will introduce a new law, and that law shall be obeyed by him only that hath a mind to it, and that will be a strange law that binds a man only to do his own pleasure. . . .

No man's opinion must be suffered to do mischief, to disturb the peace, to dishonour the government. . . . If the opinion does neither bite nor scratch, if it dwells at home in the house of understanding . . . the superior imposes no laws, and exacts no obedience, and destroys no liberty, and gives no restraint: this is the part of authority.

S.P.; VIII, 346 f.

So that you see here is the sum of affairs treated of in my text: not whether it be lawful to eat a tortoise or a mushroom, or to tread with the foot bare upon the ground within the octaves of Easter. It is not here enquired whether angels be material or immaterial; or whether the dwellings of dead infants be within the air or in the regions of the earth. The enquiry here is, whether we are to be Christians or no? whether we are to live good lives or no? *F.L.P.; VIII, 396.*

A man may do holy things unholily. *S.G.H.; I, 116.*

We are bound to obey human laws, but not bound to think the laws we live under are the most prudent constitutions in the world.

G.E. (*Pt. i, § v*)*; II, 109.*

A disproportionate instrument . . . makes the effect impossible both in nature and morality. Can a man bind a thought with chains, or carry imaginations in the palm of his hand? Can the beauty of the peacock's train or the estrich [*sic*] plume be delicious to the palate and the throat? Does the hand intermeddle with the joys of the heart, or darkness that hides the naked make him warm? *Wor. Com.* (*intro.*)*; VIII, 7.*

Although they that are dead some ages before we were born have a reverence due to them, yet more is due to truth that shall never die:

and God is not wanting to our industry any more than to theirs. . . . I must go after truth wherever it is. *D.J.; VII, 519.*

The ancients were nearer to the fountains apostolical, their stream was less puddled, their thread was not fine but plain and strong, they were troubled with fewer heresies; they were not so wittily mistaken as we have been since; they had better and more firm tradition, they had passed through fewer changes, and had been blended with fewer interests; they were united under one prince, and consequently were not forced to bend their doctrines to the hostile and opposite designs of fighting and crafty kings; their questions were concerning the biggest articles of religion, and therefore such in which they could have more certainty and less deception; their piety was great, their devotion high and pregnant, their discipline regular and sincere, their lives honest, their hearts simple, their zeal was for souls; . . . saints sprung up, and one saint could know more of the secrets of Christ's kingdom, the mysteriousness of godly wisdom, than a hundred disputing sophisters. . . .

But I reckon age amongst things that are without; it enters not into the constitution of truth; and this I know, that amongst these ancients, not all their sayings are the best. And on the other side, although antiquity is a gentle prejudice and has some authority, though no certainty or infallibility; so I know that novelty is a harder prejudice, and brings along with it no authority, but yet it is not a certain condemnation. If our fathers in religion had refused every exposition of scripture that was new, we should by this time have had nothing old; but in this case what Martial said of friendships, we may say of truths: Refuse nothing only because it is new. For that which pretends to age now, was once in infancy. *Ductor (Bk. i, ch. iv); IX, 206, 208.*

Many times virtue and vice differ but one degree; and the neighbourhood is so dangerous that he who desires to secure his obedience and duty to God, will remove farther from the danger. For there is a rule of justice to which if one degree more of severity be added it degenerates into cruelty; and a little more mercy is remissness and want of discipline.
G.E. (Pt. i, § v); II, 113 f.

It is a strange industry and an importune diligence that was used by our forefathers; of all those heresies which gave them battle and employment, we have absolutely no record or monument but what themselves who are adversaries have transmitted to us; and we know that adversaries . . . are not always the best records or witnesses of such transactions. We see it now in this very age, in the present distemperatures, that parties are no good registers of the actions of the adverse side. . . .

Of the same consideration is mending of authors not to their own mind but to ours, that is, to mend them so as to spoil them; forbidding the publication of books in which there is nothing impious or against the public interest; leaving out clauses in translation . . . false reporting of disputations and conferences; burning books by the hand of the hangman. . . . It is but an illiterate policy to think that such indirect and uningenuous proceedings can among wise and free men disgrace the authors and disrepute their discourses; and I have seen that the price hath been trebled upon a forbidden or a condemned book. And some men in policy have got a prohibition, that their impression [imprint?] might be the more certainly vendible, and the author himself thought considerable. *L.P.D.; V, 357 f.*

May I not be permitted to fight for mine honour and to wipe off the stains of my reputation? honour is as dear as life, and sometimes dearer.—To this I have many things to say. For that which men in this question call honour is nothing but a reputation amongst . . . empty and ignorant souls, who count that the standard of honour which is the instrument of reprobation, as if to be a gentleman were to be no Christian. They that have built their reputation upon such societies must take new estimates of it, according as the wine, or fancy, or custom, or some great fighting person shall determine it; and whatsoever invites a quarrel is a rule of honour. But then it is a sad consideration to remember that it is accounted honour not to recede from any thing we have said or done. It is honour not to take the lie: in the meantime it is not dishonourable to lie indeed. But to be told so and not to kill him that says it, and venture my life and his too, that is a forfeiture of reputation. A mistress's favour, an idle discourse, a jest, a jealousy, a health, a gaiety, any thing must engage two lives in hazard and two souls in ruin; or else they are dishonoured. As if a life, which is so dear to a man's self, which ought to be dear to others, which all laws and wise princes and states have secured by the circumvallation of laws and penalties, which nothing but heaven can recompense for the loss of, which is the breath of God, which to preserve Christ died, the Son of God died—as if this were so contemptible a thing that it must be ventured for satisfaction of a vicious person, or a vain custom, or such a folly which a wise and a severe person had rather die than be guilty of. Honour is from him that honours. . . .

But if we be troubled for fear of new and succeeding injuries and will needs fight, and, as much as lies in us, kill our brother to prevent an injury, nothing can be more unworthy of a Christian, nothing can be more inhuman. . . . How can fighting or killing my adversary wipe off my aspersion or take off my blow, or prove that I did not lie? For it is but an ill argument to say, If I dare kill him, then I did not lie; or if I dare fight, then he struck me not. . . .

Truth is, to fight a duel is a thing that all kingdoms are bound to restrain with highest severity; it is a consociation of many of the worst acts that a person ordinarily can be guilty of; it is want of charity, of justice, of humility, of trust in God's providence; it is therefore pride, and murder, and injustice, and infinite unreasonableness; and nothing of a Christian, nothing of excuse, nothing of honour in it, if God and wise men be admitted judges of the lists. . . . Now is it a good posture for a man to die with a sword in his hand thrust at his brother's breast, with a purpose, either explicit or implicit, to have killed him? can a man die twice, that in case he miscarries and is damned for the first ill dying, he may mend his fault and die better the next time? . . . Is there no such thing as forgiving injuries, nothing of the discipline of Jesus in our spirits? are we called by the name of Christ, and have nothing in us but the spirit of Cain and Nimrod and Joab? If neither reason nor religion can rule us, neither interest nor safety can determine us, neither life nor eternity can move us, neither God nor wise men be sufficient judges of honour to us; then . . . our fall is certain, but it is cheap, base, and inglorious. And let not the vanities or the gallants of the world slight this friendly monition, rejecting it with a scorn because it is talking like a divine: it were no disparagement if they would do so too, and believe accordingly. And they would find a better return of honour in the crowns of eternity by talking like a divine than by dying like a fool. *G.E. (Pt. ii, § xii); II, 450 ff.*

Forgiving debts is a great instance of mercy and a particular of excellent relief. But to imprison men for debt, when it is certain they are not able to pay it, and by that prison will be far more disabled, is an uncharitableness next to the cruelties of savages, and at infinite distance from the mercies of the holy Jesus.

G.E. (Pt. ii, § xii); II, 462.

He that persuades his friend, that is a goat in his manners, that he is a holy and a chaste person, or that his looseness is a sign of a quick spirit, or that it is not dangerous but easily pardonable, a trick of youth, a habit that old age will lay aside as a man pares his nails—this man hath given great advantage to his friend's mischief; he hath made it grow in all dimensions of the sin till it grows intolerable and perhaps unpardonable. *S.W. (xxiv); IV, 305.*

Is that man prosperous who hath stolen a rich robe, and is in fear to have his throat cut for it, and is fain to defend it with the greatest difficulty and the greatest danger? Does not he drink more sweetly that takes his beverage in an earthen vessel than he that looks and searches into his golden chalices for fear of poison, and looks pale at every sudden noise, and sleeps in armour, and trusts nobody, and does not trust God for his safety, but does greater wickedness only to escape awhile unpunished for his former crimes? No man goes about to poison a poor man's pitcher, nor lays plots to forage his little garden made for the hospital of two bee-hives and the feasting of a few Pythagorean herb-eaters. *S.S. (x); IV, 455.*

Princes in judgment and their delegate judges must judge the causes of all persons uprightly and impartially, without any personal consideration of the power of the mighty, or the bribe of the rich, or the needs of the poor. For although the poor must fare no worse for his poverty, yet in justice he must fare no better for it.

H.L. (ch. iii); III, 125.

It is a wonder of what excellent use to the church of Rome is *Tibi dabo claves* [To you I shall give the keys]; it was spoken to Peter and none else sometimes, and therefore it concerns him and his successors only; the rest are to derive from him. And yet if you question them for their sacrament of penance and priestly absolution, then *Tibi dabo claves* comes in, and that was spoken to S. Peter, and in him to the whole college of the apostles and in them to the whole hierarchy. If you question why the pope pretends to free souls from purgatory, *Tibi dabo claves* is his warrant; but if you tell him the keys are only for binding and loosing on earth directly and in heaven consequently, and that purgatory is . . . neither earth nor heaven nor hell, and so the keys seem to have nothing to do with it, then his commission is to be enlarged by a suppletory of reason and consequences, and his keys shall unlock this difficulty. . . . And these keys shall enable him to expound scriptures infallibly, to determine questions, to preside in Councils, to dictate to all the world magisterially, to rule the church, to dispense with oaths, to abrogate laws: and if his key of knowledge will not, the key of authority shall, and *Tibi dabo claves* shall answer for all. . . . So is done with *Pasce oves* [Feed my sheep], which a man would think were a commission as innocent and guiltless of designs as the sheep in the folds are. But if it be asked why the bishop of Rome calls himself universal bishop, *Pasce oves* is his warrant; why he pretends to a power of deposing princes, *Pasce oves*, said Christ to Peter the second time; if it be demanded why also he pretends to a power of authorizing his subjects to kill him [the prince], *Pasce oves*, said Christ the third time: and *pasce* is *doce* [teach], and *pasce* is *impera* [command], and *pasce* is *occide* [kill].

L.P., V, 419 f.

If I were bound to call any man master upon earth and to believe him upon his own affirmative and authority, I would of all men least follow him that pretends he is infallible and cannot prove it.

L.P.; V, 482.

Every man is bound to follow his guide unless he believes his guide to mislead him; yet when he sees reason against his guide, it is best to follow his reason; for though in this he may fall into error, yet he will escape the sin. He may do violence to truth, but never to his own conscience; and an honest error is better than an hypocritical profession of truth. . . .

We find persons of great understanding oftentimes so amused [occupied?] with the authority of their church that it is a pity to see them sweat in answering some objections, which they know not how to do; but yet believe they must, because the church hath said it. . . .

Although accidentally and occasionally the sheep may perish by the shepherd's fault, yet that which hath the chiefest influence upon their final condition is their own act and election; . . . although we are intrusted to our guides, yet we are intrusted to ourselves too. Our guides must direct us; and yet if they fail, God hath not so left us to them but He hath given us enough to ourselves to discover their failings and our own duties in all things necessary. . . .

It is of great concernment . . . to enquire diligently whether the will of God be so as is pretended. Even our acts of understanding are acts of choice. . . . We have no way to give our wills to God in matters of belief but by our industry in searching it and examining the grounds upon which the propounders build their dictates. . . . No man speaks more unreasonably than he that denies to men the use of their reason in choice of their religion. . . . Reason and human authority are not enemies. . . . The difference is not between reason and authority, but between this reason and that, which is greater: for authority is a very good reason and is to prevail, unless a stronger comes and disarms it, but then it must give place. . . .

In plain terms, there being so many ways of arguing, so many sects, such differing interests, such variety of authority, so many pretences and so many false beliefs, it concerns every wise man to consider which is the best argument, which proposition relies upon the truest grounds. . . . Why do they cite councils and fathers? why do they allege scripture and tradition, and all this on all sides and to contrary purposes? If we must judge, then we must use our reason; if we must not judge, why do they produce evidence? Let them leave disputing and decree propositions magisterially; but then we may choose whether we will believe them or no: or if they say we must believe them, they must prove it, and tell us why. . . .

Scripture, tradition, councils, and fathers are the evidence in a question, but reason is the judge. *L.P.; V, 493-99.*

ON LIVING WITH OTHERS

Christ forbids all "anger without cause against our brother," that is, against any man.

By which not the first motions are forbidden: the twinklings of the eye, as the philosophers call them, the propassions and sudden and irresistible alterations; for it is impossible to prevent them, unless we could give ourselves a new nature, any more than we can refuse to wink with our eye when a sudden blow is offered at it, or refuse to yawn when we see a yawning sleepy person. But by . . . continual watchfulness and standing in readiness against all inadvertencies, we shall lessen the inclination. *G.E. (Pt. ii, § xii); II, 434 f.*

It is but reasonable to bear that accident patiently which God sends, since impatience does but tangle us like the fluttering of a bird in a net, but cannot at all ease our trouble or prevent the accident.

H.L. (ch. ii); III, 100.

Much speaking is sometimes necessary, sometimes useful, sometimes pleasant; and when it is none of all this, though it be tedious and imprudent, yet it is not always criminal. Such was the humour of the gentleman Martial speaks of: he was a good man, and full of sweetness and justice and nobleness, but he would read his nonsense verses to all companies, at the public games and in private feasts, in the baths and on the beds, in public and in private, to sleeping and waking people. Everyone was afraid of him, and though he was good yet he was not to be endured. *S.W. (xxii); IV, 277.*

Some men's senses are so subtile, and their perceptions so quick and full of relish, and their spirits so active, that the same load is double upon them to what it is to another person: and therefore comparing the expressions [in sickness] of the one to the silence of the other, a different judgment cannot be made concerning their patience.

H.D. (ch. iii); III, 311.

[Parents] can do no injury more afflictive to the children than to join them [in marriage] with cords of a disagreeing affection; it is like tying a wolf and a lamb, or planting the vine in a garden of coleworts. Let them be persuaded with reasonable inducements to make them willing and to choose according to the parent's wish, but at no hand let them be forced: better to sit up all night than to go to bed with a dragon.

H.L. (ch. iii, § ii); III, 128.

Curiosity after the affairs of others cannot be without envy and an evil mind. What is it to me if my neighbour's grandfather were a Syrian, or his grandmother illegitimate; or that another is indebted five thousand pounds, or whether his wife be expensive? But commonly curious persons, or (as the apostle's phrase is) "busy-bodies," are not solicitous or inquisitive into the beauty and order of a well-governed family, or after the virtues of an excellent person; but if there be any thing, for which men keep locks and bars and porters, things that blush to see the light, and either are shameful in manners or private in nature, these things are their care and their business. But if great things will satisfy our enquiry, the course of the sun and moon, the spots in their faces, the firmament of heaven, and the supposed orbs, the ebbing and flowing of the sea, are work enough for us: or if this be not, let him tell me whether the number of the stars be even or odd, and when they began to be so; since some ages have discovered new stars which the former knew not, but might have seen if they had been where now they are fixed. If these be too troublesome, search lower, and tell me why this turf this year brings forth a daisy, and the next year a plantain; why the apple bears his seed in his heart, and wheat bears it in his head: let him tell why a graft taking nourishment from a crabstock shall have a fruit more noble than its nurse and parent: let him say why the best of oil is at the top, the best of wine in the middle, and the best of honey at the bottom. . . . But these things are not such as please busy-bodies; they must feed upon tragedies, and stories of misfortunes, and crimes; and yet tell them ancient stories of the ravishment of chaste maidens or the debauchment of nations, or the extreme poverty of learned persons, or the persecutions of the old saints, or the changes of government, and sad accidents happening in royal families amongst the Arsacidae, the Caesars, the Ptolemies, these were enough to scratch the itch of knowing sad stories; but unless you tell them something sad and new, something that is done within the bounds of their own knowledge or relation, it seems tedious and unsatisfying; which shews plainly it is an evil spirit. Envy and idleness married together and begot curiosity. *H.L. (ch. ii); III, 79 f.*

[Anger] is troublesome not only to those that suffer it, but to them that behold it—there being no greater incivility of entertainment than, for the cook's fault or the negligence of the servants, to be cruel or outrageous or unpleasant in the presence of the guests.

H.L. (ch. iv); III, 200.

We are peevish if a servant does but break a glass, and patient when we have thrown an ill cast for eternity.

Unum (ch. vi); VII, 287.

Do not many men talk themselves into anger, screwing up themselves with dialogues and fancy, till they forget the company and themselves? And some men hate to be contradicted or interrupted, or to be discovered in their folly . . . and they make it worse by discourse: a long story of themselves, a tedious praise of another collaterally to do themselves advantage . . . unseasonable repetition of that which neither profits nor delights, trifling contentions about a goat's beard or the blood of an oyster, anger and animosity, spite and rage, scorn and reproach begun upon questions which concern neither of the litigants, fierce disputations, strivings for what is past and for what never shall be. These are the events of the loose and unwary tongue, which are like flies and gnats upon the margent of a pool: they do not sting like an aspic [asp] or bite deep as a bear, yet they can vex a man into a fever and impatience, and make him uncapable of rest and counsel.

S.W. (xxiii); IV, 288.

Man and wife are equally concerned to avoid all offences of each other in the beginning of their conversation. Every little thing can blast an infant blossom, and the breath of the south can shake the little rings of the vine when first they begin to curl like the locks of a new-weaned boy; but when by age and consolidation they stiffen into the hardness of a stem, and have by the warm embraces of the sun and the kisses of heaven brought forth their clusters, they can endure the storms of the north and the loud noises of a tempest, and yet never be broken. . . . After the hearts of the man and the wife are endeared and hardened by a mutual confidence and an experience longer than artifice and pretence can last, there are a great many remembrances, and some things present, that dash all little unkindnesses in pieces. . . . When it is come thus far, it is hard untwisting the knot. . . .

Let the husband and wife infinitely avoid a curious [careful?] distinction of mine and thine, for this hath caused all the laws and all the suits and all the wars in the world; let them who have but one person have also but one interest. *S.W. (xvii); IV, 216 ff.*

He that returns good for evil, a soft answer to the asperity of his enemy, kindness to injuries, lessens the contention always and sometimes gets a friend. And when he does not, he shames his enemy. . . . But look upon a person angry, peaceless, and disturbed; when he enters upon his threshold, it gives an alarm to his house, and puts them to flight or upon their defence; and the wife reckons the joy of her day is done when he returns; and the children enquire into their father's age and think his life tedious; and the servants curse privately and do their service as slaves do, only when they dare not do otherwise; and they serve him as they serve a lion: they obey his strength and fear his cruelty and despise his manners and hate his person. No man enjoys content in his family but he that is peaceful and charitable, just and loving, forbearing and forgiving, careful and provident. He that is not so, his house may be his castle, but it is manned by enemies. . . .

No wise man ever lost anything by cession; but he receives the hostility of violent persons into his embraces like a stone into a lap of wool: it rests and sits down soft and innocently. But a stone falling upon a stone makes a collision, and extracts fire, and finds no rest: and just so are two proud persons, despised by each other, contemned by all, living in perpetual dissonancies, always fighting against affronts, jealous of every person, disturbed by every accident, a perpetual storm within and daily hissings from without. *G.E. (Pt. iii, § xiii); II, 522 f., 527 f.*

Let every minister in his charge be frequent and severe against slanderers, detractors, and backbiters; for the crime of backbiting is the poison of charity and yet so common that it is passed into a proverb, "After a good dinner let us sit down and backbite our neighbours."
Rules and Advices to the Clergy; I, 108.

The remedies against anger which are prescribed by masters of spiritual life are partly taken from rules of prudence, partly from piety and more precise rules of religion. In prudence: Firstly, do not easily entertain . . . tale-bearers and reporters of other men's faults, for oftentimes we are set on fire by an *ignis fatuus,* a false flame, and an empty story. Secondly, live with peaceable people, if thou canst. Thirdly, be not inquisitive into the misdemeanours of others, or the reports which are made of you. Fourthly, find out reasons of excuse to alleviate and lessen the ignorances of a friend or carelessnesses of a servant. Fifthly, observe what object is aptest to inflame thee, and by special arts of fortification stop up the avenues to that part. . . . Sixthly, extirpate petty curiosities [carefulnesses] of apparel, lodging, diet, and learn to be indifferent in circumstances. . . . Seventhly, do not multiply secular cares and troublesome negotiations, which have variety of conversation with several humours of men and accidents of things, but frame to thyself a life simple as thou canst and free from all affectations. Eighthly, sweeten thy temper and allay the violence of thy spirit with some convenient, natural, temperate, and medicinal solaces; for some dispositions we have seen inflamed into anger and often assaulted by peevishness through immoderate fasting and inconvenient austerities. Ninthly, a gentle answer is an excellent *remora* to the progresses of anger, whether in thyself or others. For anger is like the waves of a troubled sea; when it is corrected with a soft reply, as with a little strand, it retires and leaves nothing behind it but froth and shells—no permanent mischief. Tenthly, silence is an excellent art. *G.E. (Pt. ii, § xii); II, 440.*

FRIENDSHIP AND LOVE

[Jesus] commended the poor widow's oblation of her two mites into the treasury, it being a great love in a little print; for it was all her living. *G.E. (Pt. iii, § xv); II, 604.*

When the other women were returned and saw the Lord, then they were all together admitted to the embracement. . . .

Their forward love and the passion of their religion . . . was a greater endearment of their persons to our Lord than a more sober, reserved, and less active spirit. . . . This is supported by discourse, that by passions; this is the sobriety of the apostles, the other was the zeal of the holy women. And because a strong fancy and an earnest passion, fixed upon holy objects, are the most active and forward instruments of devotion . . . therefore we find God hath made great expressions of His acceptance of such dispositions. And women and less knowing persons, and tender dispositions and pliant natures, will make up a greater number in heaven than the severe, and wary, and enquiring people, who sometimes love because they believe . . . but never believe because they love. *G.E. (Pt. iii, § xvi); II, 723.*

"That love that can cease was never true." . . . [Love] contains in it all sweetness, and all society, and all felicity, and all prudence, and all wisdom. For there is nothing can please a man without love; and if a man be weary of the wise discourses of the apostles, and of the innocency of an even and private fortune, or hates peace or a fruitful year, he hath reaped thorns and thistles from the choicest flowers of paradise—"for nothing can sweeten felicity itself, but love." *S.W. (xviii); IV, 224*

Charity itself, which is the vertical top of all religion, is nothing else but an union of joys concentred in the heart, and reflected from all the angles of our life and entercourse. It is a rejoicing in God, a gladness in our neighbour's good, a pleasure in doing good, a rejoicing with him; and without love we cannot have any joy at all. It is this that makes children to be a pleasure, and friendship to be so noble and divine a thing. *S.W. (xxiii); IV, 291.*

Poor Adam, being banished and undone, went and lived a sad life in the mountains of India, and turned his face and his prayers towards Paradise. Thither he sent his sighs, to that place he directed his devotions; there was his heart now where his felicity sometimes had been. *S.S. (xxv); IV, 632.*

Fear is stronger than death, and love is more prevalent [prevailing] than fear, and kindness is the greatest endearment of love. . . . Let us take heed; for mercy is like a rainbow which God set in the clouds to remember mankind: it shines here as long as it is not hindered. But we must never look for it after it is night, and it shines not in the other world. If we refuse mercy here, we shall have justice to eternity.

S.S. (xxvii); IV, 672.

An old friend is like old wine, which when a man hath drunk, he doth not desire new, because he saith the old is better. But every old friend was new once; and if he be worthy, keep the new one till he become old.

After all this, treat thy friend nobly, love to be with him . . . never dissemble with him, never despise him, never leave him. Give him gifts and upbraid him not, and refuse not his kindnesses, and be sure never to despise the smallness . . . of them. "A gift," saith Solomon, "fasteneth friendships"; for as an eye that dwells long upon a star must be refreshed with lesser beauties and strengthened with greens and looking-glasses, lest the sight become amazed with too great a splendour; so must the love of friends sometimes be refreshed . . . lest by striving to be too divine it become less humane: it must be allowed its share of both: it is humane in giving pardon and fair construction, and openness and ingenuity, and keeping secrets; it hath something that is divine, because it is beneficent; but much, because it is eternal. *M.F.; I, 97 f.*

Every man rejoices twice when he hath a partner of his joy. A friend shares my sorrow, and makes it but a moiety; but he swells my joy, and makes it double. For so two channels divide the river, and lessen it into rivulets, and make it fordable, and apt to be drunk up at the first revels of the Sirian star; but two torches do not divide, but increase the flame. And though my tears are the sooner dried up when they run upon my friend's cheeks in the furrows of compassion, yet when my flame hath kindled his lamp we unite the glories and make them radiant, like the golden candlesticks that burn before the throne of God, because they shine by numbers, by unions, and confederations of light and joy. *S.S. (xxvi); IV, 652.*

No man can tell but he that loves his children how many delicious accents make a man's heart dance in the pretty conversation of those dear pledges; their childishness, their stammering, their little angers, their innocence, their imperfections, their necessities, are so many little emanations of joy and comfort to him that delights in their persons and society; but he that loves not his wife and children feeds a lioness at home, and broods a nest of sorrows. *S.W. (xviii); IV, 224.*

GOD'S FAMILY, THE WORLD

No man can make another man to be his slave unless he hath first enslaved himself to life and death, to pleasure or pain, to hope or fear: command these passions, and you are freer than the Parthian kings.
H.L. (ch. ii); III, 87.

Give, looking for nothing again; that is, without consideration of future advantages. Give to children, to old men, to the unthankful and the dying, and to those you shall never see again. . . . And if you converse in hospitals and almshouses and minister with your own hand what your heart hath first decreed, you will find your heart endeared and made familiar with the needs and with the persons of the poor, those excellent images of Christ. *H.L. (ch. iv); III, 191.*

If you please in charity to visit a hospital, which is indeed a map of the whole world, there you shall see . . . the ruins of human nature; bodies laid up in heaps like the bones of a destroyed town; men whose souls seem to be borrowed, and are kept there by art and the force of medicine, whose miseries are so great that few people have charity or humanity enough to visit them, fewer have the heart to dress them; and we pity them in civility or with a transient prayer, but we do not feel their sorrows by the mercies of a religious pity. *H.D. (ch. i); III, 286.*

I remember it was reported of St. Paul the hermit, scholar of St. Anthony, that having once asked whether Christ or the old prophets were first, he grew so ashamed of his foolish question that he spake not a word for three years following. *S.W. (xxii); IV, 282.*

A man hears the precepts of God enjoining us to give alms of all we possess; he readily obeys with much cheerfulness and alacrity, and his charity like a fair-spreading tree looks beauteously. But there is a canker at the heart. The man blows a trumpet to call the poor together and hopes the neighbourhood will take notice of his bounty. Nay, he gives alms privately and charges no man to speak of it, and yet hopes by some accident or other to be praised both for his charity and humility. And if by chance the fame of his alms comes abroad, it is but his duty to "let his light so shine before men that God may be glorified," and some of our neighbours be relieved, and others edified. *S.S. (vii); IV, 417.*

Children choose bread efformed in the image of a bird or man rather than a loaf plucked rudely from the baker's lump; and a golden fish rather than an artless ingot: because reason and art being mingled with it, it entertains more faculties and pleases on more sides.

Unum (ch. v); VII, 150.

It is good for a man to begin. The clown that stands by a river side expecting [waiting] till all the water be run away, may stay long enough before he gets to the other side. He that will not begin to live well till he hath answered all objections and hath no lusts to serve, no more appetites to please, shall never arrive at happiness in the other world. Be wise, and begin betimes. *Unum (ch. v); VII, 188.*

The two disciples that went to Emmaus saw Him, talked with Him, ate with Him, and they ran and told it: they told true, but nobody believed them. Then S. Peter saw Him, but he was not yet got into the chair of the Catholic Church; they did not think him infallible, and so they believed him not at all. *F.L.P.; VIII, 398.*

I am partly of opinion that the church of Rome is not willing to call the Collyridians heretics for offering a cake to the Virgin Mary, unless she also will run the hazard of the same sentence for offering candles to her; and that they will be glad with S. Austin [Augustine] to excuse the Tertullianists for picturing God in a visible corporal representment. And yet these sects are put in the black book by Epiphanius and S. Austin, and Isidore respectively. I remember also that the *Osseni* are called heretics because they refused to worship towards the east; and yet in that dissent I find not the malignity of a heresy nor anything against an article of faith or good manners. . . . It were hard, if they were otherwise pious men and true believers, to send them to hell for such a trifle. *L.P., V, 393.*

Humility is despised in substance, but courted and admired in effigy. . . . To prove that we are extremely proud in the midst of all this pageantry, we should be extremely angry at any man that should say we are proud; and that's a sure sign we are so. And in the midst of all our arts to seem humble, we use devices to bring ourselves into talk; we thrust ourselves into company, we listen at doors, and, like the great beards in Rome that pretended philosophy and strict life, "we walk by the obelisk," and meditate in piazzas, that they that meet us may talk of us, and they that follow may cry out, "Behold, there goes an excellent man!" He is very prudent, or very learned, or a charitable person, or a good housekeeper, or at least very humble. *S.S. (viii); IV, 426 f.*

I have seen a young and healthful person warm and ruddy under a poor and a thin garment, when at the same time an old rich person hath been cold and paralytic under a load of sables and the skins of foxes. It is the body that makes the clothes warm, not the clothes the body; and the spirit of a man makes felicity and content, not any spoils of a rich fortune wrapt about a sickly and an uneasy soul. *S.S. (x); IV, 455.*

The tables of the Lord, like the Delian altars, must not be defiled with blood and death, with anger and revenge, with wrath and indignation. . . . The blood of the cross was the last that was to have been shed. The laws can shed more, but nothing else. For by remembering and representing the effusion of blood, not by shedding it, our expiation is now perfected and complete, but nothing hinders it more than the spirit of war and death—not only by the emissions of the hand or the apertures of a wound, but by the murder of the tongue, and the cruelties of the heart, or by an unpeaceable disposition. . . .

God who made all things by His power, does preserve them by His love; and by union and society of parts every creature is preserved. . . . War is one of God's greatest plagues: and therefore when God in this holy sacrament pours forth the greatest effusion of His love, peace in all capacities, and in all dimensions, and to all purposes, He will not endure that they should come to these love feasts who are unkind to their brethren, quarrelsome with their neighbours, implacable to their enemies, apt to contentions, hard to be reconciled, soon angry, scarcely appeased. These are dogs, and must not come within the holy place, where God who is the "congregating father," and Christ the great minister of peace, and the holy Spirit of love, are present in mysterious symbols and most gracious communications.

Wor. Com. (ch. iv); VIII, 119.

The church is not a chimera, not a shadow, but a company of men believing in Jesus Christ. *L.P.; V, 492.*

Suppose a man gets all the world:

What is it that he gets? It is a bubble and a fantasm, and hath no reality beyond a present transient use; a thing that is impossible to be enjoyed because its fruits and usages are transmitted to us by parts and by succession; . . . he is so far from possessing all its riches that he does not so much as know of them, nor understand the philosophy of her minerals. . . .

Can the greatest prince enclose the sun and set one little star in his cabinet for his own use, or secure to himself the gentle and benign influence of any one constellation? Are not his subjects' fields bedewed with the same showers that water his gardens of pleasure? . . .

Unless he hath an eye like the sun and a motion like that of a thought, and a bulk as big as one of the orbs of heaven, the pleasures of his eye can be no greater than to behold the beauty of a little prospect from a hill, or to look upon the heap of gold packed up in a little room, or to dote upon a cabinet of jewels, better than which there is no man that sees at all but sees every day. For, not to name the beauties and sparkling diamonds of heaven, a man's, or a woman's, or a hawk's eye, is more beauteous and excellent than all the jewels of his crown. And when we remember that a beast, who hath quicker senses than a man, yet hath not so great delight in the fruition of any object (because he wants understanding and the power to make reflex acts upon his perception), it will follow that understanding and knowledge is the greatest instrument of pleasure, and he that is most knowing hath a capacity to become happy which a less knowing prince or a rich person hath not. *S.S.* (*xviii*); *IV, 549 ff.*

There are amongst us such tender stomachs that cannot endure milk but can very well digest iron; consciences so tender that a ceremony is greatly offensive, but rebellion is not; a surplice drives them away as a bird affrighted with a man of clouts, but their consciences can suffer them to despise government, and speak evil of dignities, and curse all that are not of their opinion, and disturb the peace of kingdoms.

S.P.; VIII, 337.

When a gentleman was commending Dr. Fisher, bishop of Rochester, his great pains in the confutation of Luther's books, the wise prelate said heartily that he wished he had spent all that time in prayer and meditation which he threw away upon such useless wranglings.

Ductor (*pref.*); *IX, xiii.*

Use not to reprove thy brother for every thing, but for great things only: for this is the office of a tutor, not of a friend. . . . When the friend of Philotimus the physician came to him to be cured of a sore finger, he told him, *Heus tu, non tibi cum reduvia est negotium* [Ho, you! the trouble's not with your hangnail]; he let his finger alone and told him that his liver was impostumate [ulcered]. And he that tells his friend that his countenance is not grave enough in the church when it may be the man is an atheist, offers him a cure that will do him no good. *S.W.* (*xxv*); *IV, 317.*

We may as well be refreshed by a clean and a brisk discourse as by the air of Campanian wines; and our faces and heads may as well be anointed and look pleasant with wit and friendly entercourse as with the fat of the balsam-tree. And such a conversation no wise man ever did, or ought to reprove. But when the jest hath teeth and nails, biting or scratching our brother, when it is loose and wanton, when it is unseasonable . . . then it is the drunkenness of the soul and makes the spirit fly away. . . .

The tongue of a babbler may crush a man's bones or break his fortune upon her own wheel. *S.W.* (*xxiii*); *IV, 292 f.*

[No commotions] are so sharp, so dangerous and intestine as those which are stirred by religion . . . the changes of religion being most commonly the most desperate paroxysms that can happen in a sickly state. Which Leontius bishop of Antioch expressed prettily by an emblem; for stroking of his old white head, he said, "When this snow is dissolved, a great deal of dirty weather would follow": meaning, when the old religion should be questioned and discountenanced, the new religions would bring nothing but trouble and unquietness.

Ductor (Bk. iii, ch. iii); X, 211.

There is hardly any orator but you may find occasion to praise something of him . . . so may men praise their preacher: he speaks pertinently, or he contrives wittily, or he speaks comely, or the man is pious, or charitable, or he hath a good text, or he speaks plainly, or he is not tedious, or if he be he is at least industrious, or he is the messenger of God and that will not fail us, and let us love him for that. And we know those that love can easily commend any thing, because they like every thing. And they say fair men are like angels, and the black are manly, and the pale look like honey and the stars, and the crook-nosed are like the sons of kings; and if they be flat, they are gentle and easy; and if they be deformed they are humble and not to be despised, because they have upon them the impresses of divinity, and they are the sons of God. *S.S.D.; IV, 328.*

All the actions of a holy life do constitute the mass and body of all those instruments whereby God is pleased to glorify Himself. For if God is glorified in the sun and moon, in the rare fabric of the honeycombs, in the discipline of bees, in the economy of pismires [ants], in the little houses of birds, in the curiosity of an eye (God being pleased to delight in those little images and reflexes of Himself from those pretty mirrors, which, like a crevice in a wall, through a narrow perspective transmit the species of a vast excellency): much rather shall God be pleased to behold Himself in the glasses of our obedience, in the emissions of our will and understanding. *S.S. (v); IV, 382.*

Though the causes of our calamities are many times great secrets of Providence, yet suppose the poverty of the man was the effect of his prodigality or other baseness; it matters not as to our duty how he came into it, but where he is. *G.E. (Pt. ii, § xii); II, 461.*

God enkindles charity upon a variety of means and instruments, by a thought, by a chance, by a text of scripture, by a natural tenderness, by the sight of a dying or a tormented beast. *G.E. (Pt. ii, § x); II, 295.*

Childhood is so tender and yet so unwary; so soft to all the impressions of chance and yet so forward to run into them, that God knew there could be no security without the care and vigilance of an angel-keeper. *F.C.C.; VIII, 432.*

[The Countess of Carbery] had not very much of the forms and outsides of godliness, but she was hugely careful for the power of it, for the moral, essential, and useful parts; such which would make her be, not seem to be, religious. *F.C.C.; VIII, 445.*

He that gives alms to the poor, takes Jesus by the hand.
G.E. (exhortation); II, 46.

There is an universal crust of hypocrisy that covers the face of the greatest part of mankind. Their religion consists in forms and outsides, and serves reputation or a design, but does not serve God.
S.S. (xxiii); IV, 610.

In this great storm which hath dashed the vessel of the church all in pieces, I have been cast upon the coast of Wales, and in a little boat thought to have enjoyed that rest and quietness which in England in a greater I could not hope for. Here I cast anchor, and thinking to ride safely, the storm followed me with so impetuous violence that it broke a cable, and I lost my anchor. And here again I was exposed to the mercy of the sea and the gentleness of an element that could neither distinguish things nor persons. . . . And now since I have come ashore, I have been gathering a few sticks to warm me, a few books to entertain my thoughts and divert them from the perpetual meditation of my private troubles and the public dyscrasy [general bad health]. . .

I had this only advantage besides, that I have chosen a subject in which, if my own reason does not abuse me, I needed no other books or aids than what a man carries with him on horseback: I mean the common principles of Christianity. . . . God is our common Master; we are all fellow-servants, and not the judge of each other in matters of conscience or doubtful disputation. *L.P.D.; V, 341, 343 f.*

SERVICE OF GOD

The counsels of religion are not to be applied to the distempers of the soul as men used to take hellebore, but they must dwell together with the spirit of a man, and be twisted about his understanding forever: they must be used like nourishment, that is by a daily care and meditation, not like a single medicine and upon the actual pressure of a present necessity. *H.L.D.; III, 4.*

God provides the good things of the world to serve the needs of nature by the labours of the ploughman, the skill and pains of the artisan, and the dangers and traffic of the merchant. These men are in their calling the ministers of the divine providence and the stewards of the creation, and servants of a great family of God, the world. . . . So that no man can complain that his calling takes him off from religion: his calling itself and his very worldly employment in honest trades and offices is a serving of God. *H.L. (ch. i); III, 9 f.*

"Faith is a certain image of eternity; all things are present to it, things past and things to come are all so before the eyes of faith," that he in whose eye that candle is enkindled beholds heaven as present, and sees how blessed a thing it is to die in God's favour and to be chimed to our grave with the music of a good conscience. Faith converses with the angels and antedates the hymns of glory: every man that hath this grace is as certain that there are glories for him if he perseveres in duty, as if he had heard and sung the thanksgiving-song for the blessed sentence of domesday. And therefore it is no matter if these things are separate and distant objects; none but children and fools are taken with the present trifle, and neglect a distant blessing of which they have credible and believed notices. Did the merchant see the pearls and the wealth he designs to get in the trade of twenty years? And is it possible that a child should, when he learns the first rudiments of grammar, know what excellent things there are in learning, whither he designs his labour and his hopes? We labour for that which is uncertain, and distant, and believed, and hoped for with many allays, and seen with diminution and a troubled ray. . . . [Faith] will, if we let it do its first intention, chastise our errors, and discover our follies; it will make us ashamed of trifling interests and violent prosecutions, of false principles and the evil disguises of the world; and then our nature will return to the innocence and excellency in which God first estated it: that is, our flesh will be a servant of the soul, and the soul a servant to the spirit.

S.W. (x); IV, 134.

We cannot believe aright . . . unless we live aright, for our faith is put upon the account just as it is made precious by charity. According to that rare saying of St. Bartholomew, recorded by the supposed St. Denis, "Charity is the greatest and the least theology"; all our faith, that is, all our religion, is completed in the duties of universal charity. As our charity or our manner of living is, so is our faith. *G.E. (Pt. ii, § x); II, 300.*

It is in some circumstances and from some persons more secure to conceal visions and those heavenly gifts which create estimations among men, than to publish them, which may possibly minister to vanity. And those exterior graces may do God's work though no observer note them but the person for whose sake they are sent: like rain falling in uninhabited valleys, where no eye observes showers, yet the valleys laugh and sing to God in their refreshment without a witness.

G.E. (Pt. i, § ii); II, 60.

We must take heed that we do not reckon religion and orders of worshipping only to be the "things of God," and all other duties to be the "things of the world," for it was a pharisaical device to cry "Corban"* and to refuse to relieve their aged parents. It is good to give to a church, but it is better to give to the poor; and though they must be both provided for, yet in cases of dispute mercy carries the cause against religion and the temple. *S.W. (xiii); IV, 164.*

Plain easy people of the laity that cannot prove Christianitv by any demonstrations, but by that of a holy life and obedience unto death: they believe it so, that they put all their hopes upon it, and will most willingly prove it again by dying for it, if God shall call them. This is one of the excellencies of faith. *Ductor (Bk. i, ch. ii); IX, 52.*

When Dorcas died, the apostle came to see the dead corpse, and the friends of the deceased expressed their grief and their love by shewing the coats that she, whilst she lived, wrought with her own hands. She was a good needle-woman . . . and the apostle himself was not displeased with their little sermons. *F.L.P.; VIII, 407.*

The instances of His piety were the actions of a very holy, but of an ordinary life; and we may observe this difference in the story of Jesus from ecclesiastical writings of certain beatified persons, whose life is told rather to amaze us and to create scruples, than to lead us in the evenness and serenity of a holy conscience. Such are the prodigious penances of Simeon Stylites, the abstinence of the Religious retired into

* The Temple treasury at Jerusalem.

the mountain Nitria, but especially the stories of later saints, in the midst of a declining piety and aged Christendom, where persons are represented holy by way of idea and fancy. . . . Yet in His external actions . . . He did so converse with men, that men, after that example, might forever converse with Him. . . . Jesus, who intended Himself the example of piety, did in manners as in the rule of faith, which, because it was propounded to all men, was fitted to every understanding: it was true, necessary, short, easy, and intelligible. *G.E. (exhortation); II, 41 f.*

In the law, God gave His spirit . . . in small proportions, like the dew upon Gideon's fleece; a little portion was wet sometimes with the dew of heaven when all the earth besides was dry. And the Jews called it *filiam vocis,* "the daughter of a voice," still, and small, and seldom, and that by secret whispers, and sometimes inarticulate, by way of enthusiasm rather than of instruction. And God spake by the prophets, transmitting the sound as through an organ pipe, things which themselves oftentimes understood not. But in the gospel the Spirit is given without measure . . . falling like the tears of the balsam of Judea upon the foot of the plant, upon the lowest of the people. . . . [It] is now not the "daughter of a voice" but the mother of many voices, of divided tongues and united hearts, of the tongues of prophets and the duty of saints, of the sermons of apostles and the wisdom of governors . . . so that old men and young men, maidens and boys, the scribe and the unlearned, the judge and the advocate, the priest and the people, are full of the Spirit if they belong to God. Moses's wish is fulfilled, and all the Lord's people are prophets in some sense or other. *S.S. (i); IV, 336 f.*

St. Lewis the king having sent Ivo bishop of Chartres on an embassy, the bishop met a woman on the way, grave, sad, fantastic, and melancholy, with fire in one hand and water in the other. He asked what those symbols meant; she answered, My purpose is with fire to burn paradise, and with my water to quench the flames of hell, that men may serve God without the incentives of hope and fear, and purely for the love of God.

S.S. (xii); IV, 477.

A moral life is not a distinct life from a theological, but a part of it, and that Christian which is just to his neighbour, and sober and temperate in his life, hath done some part of a theological and religious life. . . . To undervalue the good lives of Christians by saying they are only good moral men, because they are not of such a sect, when they do those good actions in obedience to the laws of Jesus Christ, is a profane device to advance faction and discountenance piety. . . .

Our piety must be universal, our morality must be entire, and then the good moral man shall go to God, when the religious man (as he accounts himself) shall never see Him.

And indeed one of the greatest dangers of miscarrying is in actions and undertakings and intermixtures spiritual. For besides that the whole institution of a spiritual life is a nice and a busy thing, the purgative way* being troublesome and austere, the illuminative being mysterious and apt to be abused, the unitive way not to be understood till it be felt and therefore liable to all miscarriages, as not to be guided by rule—besides all this, I say, spiritual vices are most dangerous and yet most apt to insinuate themselves in the actions of greatest perfections, and when they are mixed, 'tis extremely difficult to discern them and make a separation. *G.H.; I, 125 f.*

A man may very well live in the world and yet serve God; and if he be hindered by the world, it is not directly that, but something else by which the cure must be effected. *Wor. Com. (ch. v); VIII, 168.*

Do not despise external religion, because it may be sincere, and do not rely upon it wholly, because it may be counterfeit; but do you preach both, and practice both. *M.D.; VIII, 535.*

Indeed there is scarce anything but what is written in scripture that can with any confidence of argument pretend to derive from the apostles except rituals and manners of ministration; but no doctrines or speculative mysteries are so transmitted to us by so clear a current that we may see a visible channel, and trace it to the primitive fountains. *L.P.; V, 436.*

Music one way affects the soul, and witty discourses another, and joyful tidings a way differing from both the former; so the operations of the sacrament are produced by an energy of a nature entirely differing from all things else. But however it is done, the thing that is done is this: no grace is there improved but what we bring along with us; no increases but what we exercise: we must bring faith along with us and God will increase our faith; we must come with charity and we shall go away with more. *Wor. Com. (ch. i); VIII, 45.*

In every action of religion God expects such a warmth and a holy fire to go along that it may be able to enkindle the wood upon the altar and consume the sacrifice; but God hates an indifferent spirit. Earnestness and vivacity, quickness and delight, perfect choice of the service and a delight in the prosecution, is all that the spirit of a man can yield towards his religion. The outward work is the effect of the body; but if a man does it heartily and with all his mind, then religion hath wings and moves upon wheels of fire. *S.W. (xiii); IV, 155.*

* The first step in mystical education, followed by the illuminative and the unitive.

If he [the devil] can but make men unwilling to pray, or to pray coldly or to pray seldom, he secures his interest and destroys the man's. And it is infinitely strange that he can and doth prevail so much in this so unreasonable temptation; the mourning prophet complained, "there was a cloud passed between heaven and the prayer of Judah"; a little thing, God knows. It was a wall which might have been blown down with a few hearty sighs and a few penitential tears . . . but so the devil prevails often; "he claps a cloud between." Some little objection: "a stranger is come"; or "my head aches"; or "the church is too cold"; or "I have letters to write"; or "I am not disposed"; or "it is not yet time"; or "the time is past." . . . The smallest article of objection managed and conducted by the devil's arts, and meeting with a wretchless, careless, indevout spirit, is a lion in the way and a deep river; it is impassable, and it is impregnable. *S.W. (xiv); IV, 169 f.*

Probable arguments are like little stars, every one of which will be useless as to our conduct and enlightening; but when they are tied together by order and vicinity, by the finger of God and the hand of an angel, they make a constellation, and are not only powerful in their influence, but like a bright angel to guide and to enlighten our way. And although the light is not great as the light of the sun or moon, yet mariners sail by their conduct; and though with trepidation and some danger, yet very regularly they enter into the haven.

Ductor (Bk. i, ch. iv); IX, 154.

He that is warm today and cold to-morrow . . . he is *duplicis animi*, as St. James calls him, "of a doubtful mind." For religion is worth as much to-day as it was yesterday, and that cannot change though we do; and if we do, we have left God. . . . This fire must never go out, but it must be like the fire of heaven; it must shine like the stars: though sometimes covered with a cloud or obscured by a greater light, yet they dwell forever in their orbs, and walk in their circles and observe their circumstances, but go not out by day nor night, and set not when kings die, nor are extinguished when nations change their government: so must the zeal of a Christian be. *S.W. (xiii); IV, 166.*

What have your people to do whether Christ's body be in the sacrament by consubstantiation or transubstantiation; whether purgatory be in the centre of the earth or in the air, or any where or nowhere? And who but a mad man would trouble their heads with the intangled links of the fanatic chain of predestination? . . . Is it not a shame that the people should be filled with sermons against ceremonies, and declamations against a surplice, and tedious harangues against the poor airy sign of the cross in baptism? . . . If S. Paul or S. Anthony, S. Basil or S. Ambrose, if any of the primitive confessors or glorious martyrs should awake from within their curtains of darkness and find men thus striving against government for the interest of disobedience, and labouring for nothings, and preaching all day for shadows and moonshine . . . if, I say, S. Paul or S. Anthony should see such a light, they would not know the meaning of it, nor of what religion the country were, nor from whence they had derived their new nothing of an institution. *M.D.; VIII, 532 f.*

No rational man can think that any ceremony can make a spiritual change without a spiritual act of him that is to be changed; nor work by way of nature or by charm, but morally, and after the manner of reasonable creatures. *H.D.D.; III, 261.*

Can prayers for a dead man do him more good than when he was alive? If all his days the man belonged to death and the dominion of sin, and from thence could not be recovered by sermons . . . by confessions and absolutions, by prayers and advocations, by external ministries and internal acts, it is but too certain that his lamp cannot then be furnished. *H.D.D.; III, 262.*

A man cannot be an excellent lawyer without twenty years' skill and practice, besides excellency of natural endowments, and yet can be an excellent teacher and guide in all cases of conscience, merely with opening his mouth and rubbing his forehead hard. . . . They that have not the wisdom of prophets and wise men cannot easily be brought to know the degrees of distance between the others' wisdom and their own ignorance. To know that there is great learning beyond us is a great part of learning. *D.I.O.M.* (§ *iii*) *; I, 22.*

Be more careful to establish a truth than to reprove an error; . . . men will be less apt to reprove your truth when they are not engaged to defend their own propositions against you. Men stand upon their guard when you proclaim war against their doctrine. . . .

If any man have a revelation or a discovery of which thou knowest nothing but by his preaching, be not too quick to condemn it; not only lest thou discourage his labour and stricter enquiries in the search of truth, but lest thou also be a fool upon record; for so is every man that hastily judges what he slowly understands. Is it not a monument of a lasting reproach that one of the popes of Rome condemned the bishop of Salzburg for saying that there were *antipodes?* . . . and posterity will certainly make themselves very merry with the wise sentences made lately at Rome against Galileo. . . .

But above all things nothing so much will reproach your doctrine as if you preach it in a railing dialect; we have had too much of that within these last thirty years. . . . You begin to read chapters and you expound them to our injuries; you comment upon the gospel, and revile your brethren that are absent; you imprint hatred and enmity in your people's hearts and you teach them war when you pretend to make them saints. *M.D.; VIII, 535 f., 537 f.*

A repentance upon our death-bed is like washing the corpse; it is cleanly and civil but makes no change deeper than the skin.

H.D. (*ch. iv*); *III, 372.*

He that means to gain a soul must not make his sermon an ostentation of his eloquence, but the law of his own life. If a grammarian should speak solecisms or a musician sing like a bittern, he becomes ridiculous for offending in the faculty he professes. So it is in them who minister to the conversion of souls; if they fail in their own life when they profess to instruct another, they are defective in their proper part and are unskillful to all their purposes. . . . For good counsel seems to be unhallowed when it is reached forth by an impure hand, and he can ill be believed by another whose life so confutes his rules that it is plain he does not believe himself. *S.S.* (*xxi*); *IV, 588.*

It were very well . . . that we would be careful to use all those ministries, and be earnest for all those doctrines, which . . . are apt to produce holiness and severe living. It is no matter whether by these arts any sect or name be promoted; it is certain Christian religion would, and that's the real interest of us all. *Unum* (*pref.*); *VII, 16.*

EARTH, AIR, AND WATER

He that is merry and airy at shore when he sees a sad and a loud tempest on the sea, or dances briskly when God thunders from heaven, regards not when God speaks to all the world, but is possessed with a firm immodesty. *H.L.* (*ch. ii*); *III, 81.*

The smallest atoms that dance in all the little cells of the world are so trifling and immaterial that they cannot trouble an eye, nor vex the tenderest part of a wound where a barbed arrow dwelt; yet when by their infinite numbers (as Melissa and Parmenides affirm) they danced first into order, then into little bodies; at last they made the matter of the world: so are the little indiscretions of our life. *H.D.* (*ch. ii*); *III, 298.*

Nature makes excellent friendships; of which we observe something in social plants, growing better in each other's neighbourhood than where they stand singly. *M.F.*; *I, 86.*

Between the very vital spirits of friends and relatives there is a cognation, and they refresh each other like social plants.

S.S. (iv); IV, 380.

As the face of the waters wafting in a storm so wrinkles itself that it makes upon its forehead furrows deep and hollow like a grave, so do our great and little cares and trifles first make the wrinkles of old age, and then they dig a grave for us: and there is in nature nothing so contemptible but it may meet with us in such circumstances that it may be too hard for us in our weaknesses. And the sting of a bee is a weapon sharp enough to pierce the finger of a child or the lip of a man; and those creatures which nature hath left without weapons . . . are armed sufficiently to vex those parts of men which are left defenceless and obnoxious to a sunbeam, to the roughness of a sour grape, to the unevenness of a gravelstone, to the dust of a wheel, or the unwholesome breath of a star looking awry upon a sinner.

F.C.C.; VIII, 430 f.

[The Countess of Carbery] had a strange evenness . . . sliding toward her ocean of God and of infinity with a certain and silent motion. So have I seen a river deep and smooth passing with a still foot and a sober face, and paying to . . . the great exchequer of the sea, the prince of all the watery bodies, a tribute large and full: and hard by it a little brook skipping and making a noise upon its unequal and neighbour bottom. And after all its talking and bragged motion, it payed to its common audit no more than the revenues of a little cloud or a contemptible vessel. *F.C.C.; VIII, 447.*

Pardon of sins . . . enters upon them [persons] by little portions, and it is broken as their sighs and sleeps. But so have I seen the returning sea enter upon the strand; and the waters, rolling towards the shore, throw up little portions of the tide, and retire, as if nature meant to play and not to change the abode of waters. But still the flood crept by little steppings, and invaded more by his progressions than he lost by his retreat: and having told the number of its steps, it possesses its new portion till the angel calls it back that it may leave its unfaithful dwelling of the sand. So is the pardon of our sins: it comes by slow motions and first quits a present death, and turns, it may be, into a sharp sickness. And if that sickness prove not health to the soul, it washes off; and it may be, will dash against the rock again and proceed to take off the several instances of anger and the periods of wrath.

S.W. (viii); IV, 98.

If you thrust a jessamine there where she [nature] would have a daisy grow, or bring the tall fir from dwelling in his own country, and transport the orange or the almond-tree near the fringes of the north-star, nature is displeased, and becomes unnatural and starves her sucklings, and renders you a return less than your charge and expectation. *S.W. (xv); IV, 184.*

As the Sun of righteousness approached towards the chambers of the east, and sent the harbingers of light peeping through the curtains of the night and leading on the day of faith and brightest revelation, so God sent degrees of trouble upon wise and good men that now . . . they might be able to live in virtue even while she [the world] lived in trouble, and not reject so great a beauty because she goes in mourning, and hath a black cloud of cypress* drawn before her face.

S.S. (ix); IV, 432.

For as the sun sends forth a benign and gentle influence on the seed of plants that it may invite forth the active and plastic power from its recess and secrecy, that by rising into the tallness and dimensions of a tree it may still receive a greater and more refreshing influence from its foster-father, the prince of all the bodies of light (and in all these emanations the sun itself receives no advantage but the honour of doing benefits): so doth the almighty Father of all the creatures.

S.S. (xii); IV, 471.

I [have] seen the little purls of a spring sweat through the bottom of a bank and intenerate the stubborn pavement till it hath made it fit for the impression of a child's foot; and it was despised, like the descending pearls of a misty morning, till it had opened its way and made a stream large enough to carry away the ruins of the undermined strand, and to invade the neighbouring gardens. *S.S. (xvi); IV, 527.*

Repentance is like the sun, which enlightens not only the tops of the eastern hills, or warms the wall-fruits of Italy. It makes the little balsam tree to weep precious tears with staring upon its beauties; it produces rich spices in Arabia, and warms the cold hermit in his grot, and calls the religious man from his dorter [dormitory] in all the parts of the world where holy religion dwells. At the same time it digests the American gold and melts the snows from the Riphaean mountains, because he darts his rays in every portion of the air; and the smallest atom that dances in the air is tied to a little thread of light, which by equal emanations fills all the capacities of every region. So is repentance; it scatters its beams and holy influences. . . . But the little drops of a beginning sorrow, and the pert resolution to live better, never passing into act and habit . . . are but like the sudden fires of the night, which

* A curled silk or cotton gauze, usually used for mourning.

glare for a while within a little continent of air big enough to make a fire-ball or the revolution of a minute's walk. *Unum (ch. x); VII, 478.*

When a little water is spilt from a full vessel and falls into its enemy dust, it curls itself into a drop and so stands equally armed in every point of the circle, dividing the forces of the enemy, that by that little union it may stand as long as it can; but if it be dissolved into flatness it is changed into the nature and possession of the dust.

Wor. Com. (ch. iv); VIII, 119.

The friends and disciples of the holy Jesus, having devoutly composed His body to burial, anointed it, washed it, and condited it with spices and perfumes, laid it in a sepulchre hewn from a rock in a garden; which, saith Euthymius, was therefore done to represent that we were by this death returned to paradise. . . . Here He finished the work of His passion, as He had begun it, in a garden. *G.E. (Pt. iii, § xvi); II, 720.*

John came forth from his solitude and served God in societies. He served God and the content of his own spirit by his conversing with angels and dialogues with God, so long as he was in the wilderness . . . but now himself, that tried both, was best able to judge which state of life was of greatest advantage and perfection.

"In his solitude [said Origen] he did breathe more pure inspiration, heaven was more open, God was more familiar."

G.E. (Pt. i, § viii); II, 167.

The life of a man comes upon him slowly and insensibly. But as when the sun approaches towards the gates of the morning, he first opens a little eye of heaven, and sends away the spirits of darkness, and gives light to a cock, and calls up the lark to matins, and by and by gilds the fringes of a cloud, and peeps over the eastern hills, thrusting out his golden horns . . . and still while a man tells the story, the sun gets up higher, till he shews a fair face and a full light, and then he shines one whole day, under a cloud often, and sometimes weeping great and little showers, and sets quickly: so is a man's reason and his life. *H.D. (ch. i); III, 277.*

There is nothing greater for which God made our tongues, next to reciting His praises, than to minister comfort to a weary soul. . . . So have I seen the sun kiss the frozen earth which was bound up with the images of death and the colder breath of the north; and then the waters break from their enclosures and melt with joy and run in useful

channels; and the flies do rise again from their little graves in walls, and dance awhile in the air to tell that there is joy within, and that the great mother of creatures will open the stock of her new refreshment, become useful to mankind, and sing praises to her Redeemer: so is the heart of a sorrowful man under the discourses of a wise comforter.
S.W. (xxv); IV, 314.

TIME

Men live in their course and by turns. Their light burns a while, and then it burns blue and faint, and men go to converse with spirits and then they reach the taper to another. And as the hours of yesterday can never return again, so neither can the man whose hours they were and who lived them over once; he shall never come to live again, and live them better. . . .

[The godly] descend into their graves and shall no more be reckoned among the living; they have no concernment in all that is done under the sun. Agamemnon hath no more to do with the Turks' armies invading and possessing that part of Greece where he reigned, than had the hippocentaur who never had a being: and Cicero hath no more interest in the present evils of christendom than we have to do with his boasted discovery of Catiline's conspiracy. What is it to me that Rome was taken by the Gauls? and what is it now to Camillus if different religions be tolerated amongst us? These things that now happen concern the living. *F.C.C.; VIII, 433, 435.*

The little birds and laborious bees, who having no art and power of contrivance, no distinction of time or foresight of new necessities, yet being guided by the hand and counselled by the wisdom of the supreme Power, their Lord and ours, do things with greater niceness and exactness of art and regularity of time and certainty of effect, than the wise counsellor who, standing at the back of the prince's chair, guesses imperfectly and counsels timorously and thinks by interest.
S.W. (xxiii); IV, 287.

[Men's] pleasure dies like the time in which it danced awhile; and when the minute is gone, so is the pleasure too, and leaves no footstep but the impression of a sigh, and dwells nowhere but in the same house where you shall find yesterday. *S.S. (xx); IV, 577.*

That which I complain of is that we look upon wise men that lived long ago with so much veneration and mistake, that we reverence them not for having been wise men, but that they lived long since. But when the question is concerning authority, there must be something to build it on; a divine commandment, human sanction, excellency of spirit, and greatness of understanding, on which things all human authority is regularly built. . . . Beyond this, why the bishop of Hippo [S. Augustine] shall have greater authority than the bishop of the Canaries, *caeteris paribus,* I understand not. *L.P.; V, 487.*

Businesses intervene, and visits are made, and civilities to be rendered, and friendly compliances to be entertained, and necessities to be served; and some things thought so, which are not so. And so the time goes away, and the duty is left undone; prayers are hindered and prayers are omitted; and concerning every part of time which was once in our power, no man living can give a fair account.

Unum (ch. i); VII, 28.

We are pleased to throw away our time and are weary of many parts of it, yet are impatiently troubled when all is gone.

S.W. (xxii); IV, 281.

He had a star to illustrate His birth, but a stable for His bedchamber and a manger for His cradle. The angels sang hymns when He was born, but He was cold and cried, uneasy and unprovided. . . . He entered into a state of death, whose shame and trouble was great enough to pay for the sins of the whole world. And I shall choose to express this mystery in the words of scripture. He died not by a single or a sudden death, but He was the "Lamb slain from the beginning of the world": for He was massacred in Abel, saith St. Paulinus; . . . He was offered up in Isaac, persecuted in Jacob, betrayed in Joseph, blinded in Samson, affronted in Moses, sawed in Esay, cast into the dungeon with Jeremy. . . . It is He that is stoned in St. Stephen, flayed in the person of St. Bartholomew; He was roasted upon St. Laurence his gridiron, exposed to lions in St. Ignatius, burned in St. Polycarp, frozen in the lake where stood forty martyrs of Cappadocia. . . . Said St. Hilary, "the sacrament of Christ's death is not to be accomplished but by suffering all the sorrows of humanity." *S.S. (ix); IV, 435 f.*

Time itself is checkered with black and white; stay but till to-morrow, and your present sorrow will be weary and will lie down to rest.

S.W. (xxv); IV, 313.

Let your sleep be necessary and healthful, not idle and expensive of time, beyond the needs and conveniences of nature; and sometimes be curious to see the preparation which the sun makes when he is coming forth from his chambers of the east. *H.L. (ch. i); III, 11.*

Gather together into your spirit, and its treasure-house the memory, not only all the promises of God but also the remembrances of experience and the former senses of the divine favours, that from thence you may argue from times past to the present and enlarge to the future, and to greater blessings. For although the conjectures and expectations of hope are not like the conclusions of faith, yet they are a helmet against the scorchings of despair in temporal things, and an anchor of the soul sure and steadfast against the fluctuations of the spirit in matters of the soul. *H.L. (ch. iv); III, 154.*

It is very remarkable that God, who giveth plenteously to all creatures, (He hath scattered the firmament with stars, as a man sows corn in his fields, in a multitude bigger than the capacities of human order; He hath made so much variety of creatures, and gives us great choice of meats and drinks, although any one of both kinds would have served our needs: and so in all instances of nature) yet in the distribution of our time God seems to be strait-handed and gives it to us, not as nature gives us rivers, enough to drown us, but drop by drop, minute after minute, so that we never can have two minutes together, but He takes away one when He gives us another. This should teach us to value our time, since God so values it, and by His so small distribution of it tells us it is the most precious thing we have.
H.D. (ch. ii); III, 294.

No man at once feels the sickness of a week or of a whole day, but the smart of an instant; and still every portion of a minute feels but its proper share, and the last groan ended all the sorrow of its peculiar burden. And what minute can that be which can pretend to be intolerable? And the next minute is but the same as the last, and the pain flows like the drops of a river or the little shreds of time; and if we do but take care of the present minute, it cannot seem a great charge or a great burden. *H.D. (ch. iii); III, 315.*

God hath given to man a short time here upon earth, and yet upon this short time eternity depends. . . .

We must remember that we have a great work to do, many enemies to conquer, many evils to prevent, much danger to run through, many difficulties to be mastered, many necessities to serve, and much good to do. *H.L. (ch. i); III, 9.*

Let not your recreations be lavish spenders of your time, but choose such which are healthful, short, transient, recreative, and apt to refresh you. But at no hand dwell upon them or make them your great employment: for he that spends his time in sports and calls it recreation is like him whose garment is all made of fringes, and his meat nothing but sauces. *H.L. (ch. i); III, 13.*

Though we must not look so far off and pry abroad, yet we must be busy near at hand; we must with all arts of the spirit seize upon the present, because it passes from us while we speak and because in it all our certainty does consist. We must take our waters as out of a torrent and sudden shower, which will quickly cease dropping from above and quickly cease running in our channels here below. This instant will never return again, and yet it may be this instant will declare or secure the fortune of a whole eternity. *H.D. (ch. i); III, 275.*

DEATH AND ITS SHADOW

My lord [the Earl of Carbery], it is a great art to die well, and to be learnt by men in health, by them that can discourse and consider, by those whose understanding and acts of reason are not abated with fear or pains; . . . he that prepares not for death before his last sickness is like him that begins to study philosophy when he is going to dispute publicly in the faculty. *H.D.D.; III, 258.*

We have had no new revelation concerning it [death]; but it is ten to one but when we die we shall find the state of affairs wholly differing from all our opinions here, and that no man or sect hath guessed any thing at all of it as it is. . . .

Dead persons have religion passed upon them and a solemn reverence: and if we think a ghost beholds us, it may be we may have upon us the impressions likely to be made by love, and fear, and religion. *H.D. (ch. v); III, 454 f.*

Something is to be given to custom, something to fame, to nature and to civilities, and to the honour of the deceased friends; for that man is esteemed to die miserable for whom no friend or relative sheds a tear or pays a solemn sigh. I desire to die a "dry death," but am not very desirous to have a "dry funeral": some flowers sprinkled upon my grave would do well and comely, and a soft shower to turn those flowers into a springing memory or a fair rehearsal. . .

But that which is to be faulted in this particular is when the grief is immoderate and unreasonable. . . . It is worse yet when people by an ambitious and a pompous sorrow and by ceremonies invented for the ostentation of their grief, fill heaven and earth with exclamations and grow troublesome because their friend is happy or themselves want his company. *H.D. (ch. v); III, 446 f.*

Take away but the pomps of death, the disguises and solemn bugbears, the tinsel and the actings by candle-light, and proper and fantastic ceremonies, the minstrels and the noise-makers, the women and the weepers, the swoonings and the shriekings, the nurses and the physicians, the dark room and the ministers, the kindred and the watchers; and then to die is easy, ready and quitted from its troublesome circumstances. It is the same harmless thing that a poor shepherd suffered yesterday, or a maid-servant to-day. And at the same time in which you die, in that very night a thousand creatures die with you, some wise men, and many fools; and the wisdom of the first will not quit him, and the folly of the latter does not make him unable to die. *H.D. (ch. iii); III, 339.*

Death is nothing but a middle point between two lives.
F.C.C.; VIII, 438.

Death is not an action, but a whole state and condition.
H.D. (ch. iii); III, 309.

In sleep our senses are as fast bound by nature as our joints are by the grave-clothes; and unless an angel of God awaken us every morning, we must confess ourselves as unable to converse with men as we now are afraid to die and to converse with spirits. But however, death itself is no more; it is but darkness and a shadow, a rest and a forgetfulness. What is there more in death? what is there less in sleep? . . . When the cock and the lark call us up to prayer and labour, the first thing we see is an argument of our resurrection from the dead. . . .

Night and day, the sun returning to the same point of east, every change of species in the same matter, generation and corruption, the eagle renewing her youth and the snake her skin, the silk-worm and the swallows, the care of posterity and the care of an immortal name, winter and summer, the fall and spring, . . . the visions of the prophets, . . . the histories of the Jews and the narratives of Christians; . . . all join in the verification of this mystery. *F.L.P.; VIII, 402 f.*

What great matter is it if sparks fly upward, or a stone falls into a pit; if that which was combustible be burned, or that which was liquid be melted, or that which is mortal do die? It is no more than a man does every day: for every night death hath gotten possession of that day, and we shall never live that day over again. And when the last day is come, there are no more days left for us to die. And what is sleeping and waking, but living and dying? What is spring and autumn, youth and old age, morning and evening, but real images of life and death, and really the same to many considerable effects and changes? . . .

That life is not best which is longest: and when they are descended into the grave, it shall not be enquired how long they have lived, but how well. . . .

The sons and the parents, friends and relatives, are in the world like hours and minutes to a day: the hour comes, and must pass; and some stay but minutes, and they also pass, and shall never return again. But let it be considered that from the time in which a man is conceived, from that time forward to eternity he shall never cease to be: and let him die young or old, still he hath an immortal soul and hath laid down his body only for a time. . . . But he is in a more noble manner of being after death than he can be here: and the child may with more reason be allowed to cry for leaving his mother's womb for this world, than a man can for changing this world for another. *H.L. (ch. ii); III, 107 ff.*

All our life we are dying, and this minute in which I now write death divides with me, and hath got the surer part and more certain possession. . . . The age of every day [is] a beginning of death, and the night composing us to sleep bids us go to our lesser rest, because that night which is the end of the preceding day is but a lesser death. And whereas now we have died so many days, the last day of our life is but the dying so many more, and when that last day of dying will come, we know not. . . . Men are pleased to call that death which is the end of dying, when we cease to die any more.

G.E. (Pt. iii, § xv); II, 680 f.

[Death] is a thing that is no great matter in itself, if we consider that we die daily, that it meets us in every accident, that every creature carries a dart along with it and can kill us. And therefore when Lysimachus threatened Theodorus to kill him, he told him that was no great matter to do, and he could do no more than the cantharides* could: a little fly could do as much. *H.D. (ch. iii); III, 339.*

Every man . . . must put his house in order. . . . It is excellent charity to leave our will and desires clear, plain, and determinate, that contention and lawsuits may be prevented by the explicate declaration of the legacies. At last . . . let God be praised for all His graces and blessings of our life. . . . And if the condition of our sickness permits it, let our last breath expire with an act of love, that it may begin the charities of eternity, and, like a taper burnt to its lowest base, it may go out with a great emission of light. *G.E. (Pt. iii, § xv); II, 700.*

* Spanish flies.

Men are impatient of the thoughts of death. Hence come those arts of protraction and delaying the significations of old age: thinking to deceive the world, men cozen themselves, and by representing themselves youthful they certainly continue their vanity till Proserpina pull the peruke from their heads. We cannot deceive God and nature: for a coffin is a coffin, though it be covered with a pompous veil; and the minutes of our time strike on and are counted by angels, till the period comes which must cause the passing bell to give warning to all the neighbours that thou art dead, and they must be so: and nothing can excuse or retard this. *H.D. (ch. iii); III, 336.*

When God sends His angel to us with the scroll of death, let us look on it as an act of mercy . . . and lay our heads down softly and go to sleep without wrangling like babies and froward children. For a man at least gets this by death, that his calamities are not immortal.

H.D. (ch. iii); III, 338.

[In sickness] the flesh sits uneasily and dwells in sorrow; and then the spirit feels itself at ease, freed from the petulant solicitations of those passions which in health were as busy and as restless as atoms in the sun, always dancing, and always busy, and never sitting down, till a sad night of grief and uneasiness draws the veil and lets them die alone in secret dishonour. . . .

And when in sickness we forget all our knotty discourses of philosophy, and a syllogism makes our head ache, and we feel our many and loud talkings served no lasting end of the soul, no purpose that now we must abide by, and that the body is like to descend to the land where all things are forgotten; then she lays aside all her remembrances of applauses, all her ignorant confidences, and cares only to know "Christ Jesus and Him crucified," to know Him plainly, and with much heartiness and simplicity. And I cannot think this to be a contemptible advantage.

H.D. (ch. iii); III, 324 f.

There is no sickness so great but children endure it, and have natural strengths to bear them out quite through the calamity, what period soever nature hath allotted it. Indeed they make no reflections upon their sufferings and complain of sickness with an uneasy sigh or a natural groan, but consider not what the sorrows of sickness mean, and so bear it by a direct sufferance, and as a pillar bears the weight of a roof. But then why cannot we bear it so too? For this which we call a reflection upon or a considering of our sickness is nothing but a perfect instrument of trouble. . . . Poor children that endure so much have not inward supports and refreshments to bear them through it: they never heard the sayings of old men nor have been taught the principles of severe philosophy, nor are assisted with the results of a long experience, nor know they how to turn a sickness into virtue and a fever into a reward; . . . and yet nature hath in them teeth and nails enough to scratch and fight against the sickness, and by such aids as God is pleased to give them they wade through the storm and murmur not. . . . Therefore bear up; either you or I, or some man wiser, and many a woman weaker than us both, or the very children, have endured worse evil than this that is upon thee now. *H.D. (ch. iii); III, 314 f.*

At the first address and presence of sickness, stand still and arrest thy spirit that it may, without amazement or affright, consider that this was that thou lookedst for and wert always certain should happen, and that now thou art to enter into the actions of a new religion, the agony of a strange constitution; but at no hand suffer thy spirits to be dispersed with fear or wildness of thought, but stay their looseness and dispersion by a serious consideration of the present and future employment. . . . Every man when shot with an arrow from God's quiver must then draw in all the auxiliaries of reason, and know that then is the time to try his strength and to reduce the words of his religion into action, and consider that if he behaves himself weakly and timorously, he suffers nevertheless of sickness; but if he returns to health he carries along with him the mark of a coward and a fool; and if he descends into his grave, he enters into the state of the faithless and unbelievers. Let him set his heart firm upon this resolution, "I must bear it inevitably, and I will, by God's grace, do it nobly." . . .

Resolve to bear your sickness like a child, that is, without considering the evils and the pains, the sorrows and the danger; but go straight forward, and let thy thoughts cast about for nothing but how to make advantages of it by the instrument of religion. . . . He that tells his groans and numbers his sighs, and reckons one for every gripe of his belly or throb of his distempered pulse, will make an artificial sickness greater than the natural. And if thou beest ashamed that a child should bear an evil better than thou, then take his instrument and allay thy spirit with it. . . .

Be obedient to thy physician in those things that concern him, if he be a person fit to minister unto thee. . . . Use him temperately, without violent confidences; and sweetly, without uncivil distrustings, or refusing his prescriptions upon humours or impotent fear. . . .

Treat thy nurses and servants sweetly, and as it becomes an obliged and a necessitous person. Remember that thou art very troublesome to them; that they trouble not thee willingly; that they strive to do thee ease and benefit, that they wish it and sigh and pray for it, and are glad if thou likest their attendance: that whatsoever is amiss is thy disease, and the uneasiness of thy head or thy side, thy distemper or thy disaffections; and it will be an unhandsome injustice to be troublesome to them, because thou are so to thyself. *H.D. (ch. iv); III, 354 f., 357 f.*

A man is a bubble, said the Greek proverb; . . . all the world is a storm, and men rise up in their several generations like bubbles descending *a Jove pluvio,* from God and the dew of heaven, from a tear and drop of man, from nature and Providence: and some of these instantly sink into the deluge of their first parent and are hidden in a sheet of water, having had no other business in the world but to be born that they might be able to die: others float up and down two or three turns, and suddenly disappear, and give their place to others: and they that live longest upon the face of the waters are in perpetual motion, restless and uneasy; and being crushed with the great drop of a cloud sink into flatness and a froth; the change not being great, it being hardly possible it should be more a nothing than it was before. So is every man: he is born in vanity and sin; he comes into the world like morning mushrooms, soon thrusting up their heads into the air, and conversing with their kindred of the same production, and as soon they turn into dust and forgetfulness: some of them without any other interest in the affairs of the world but that they made their parents a little glad, and very sorrowful: others ride longer in the storm; it may be until seven years of vanity be expired, and then peradventure the sun shines hot upon their heads, and they fall into the shades below, into the cover of death and darkness of the grave to hide them. But if the bubble stands the shock of a bigger drop, and outlives the chances of a child, of a careless nurse, of drowning in a pail of water, of being overlaid by a sleepy servant, or such little accidents, then the young man dances like a bubble, empty and gay, and shines like a dove's neck, or the image of a rainbow, which hath no substance, and whose very imagery and colours are fantastical; and so he dances out the gaiety of his youth, and is all the while in a storm, and endures only because he is not knocked on the head by a drop of bigger rain, or crushed by the pressure of a load of indigested meat, or quenched by the disorder of an ill-placed humour: and to preserve a man alive in the midst of so many chances and hostilities, is as great a miracle as to create him; to preserve him from rushing into nothing, and at first to draw him up from nothing, were equally the issues of an almighty power. And therefore the wise men of the world have contended who shall best fit man's condition with words signifying his vanity and short abode. Homer calls a man "a leaf," the smallest, the weakest piece of a short-lived, unsteady plant: Pindar calls him "the dream of a shadow": another, "the dream of the shadow of smoke": but St. James spake by a more excellent spirit, saying, "our life is but a vapour," viz., drawn from the earth by a celestial influence; made of smoke, or the lighter parts of water, tossed with every wind, moved by the motion of a superior body, without virtue in itself, lifted up on high or left below, according as it pleases the sun its foster-father. . . . And yet the expression is one degree more made diminutive: a "vapour," and "fantastical," or a "mere appearance," and this but for a little while neither; the very dream, the phantasm disappears in a small time, "like the shadow that departeth"; or "like a tale that is told"; or "as a dream, when one waketh." A man is so vain, so unfixed, so perishing a creature, that he cannot long last in the scene of fancy: a man goes off, and is forgotten, like the dream of a distracted person. The sum of all is this: that thou art a man, than whom there is not in the world any greater instance of heights and declensions, of lights and shadows, of misery and folly, of laughter and tears, of groans and death. *H.D. (ch. i); III, 265 f.*

A man may read a sermon, the best and most passionate that ever man preached, if he shall but enter into the sepulchres of kings. In the same Escurial where the Spanish princes live in greatness and power, and decree war or peace, they have wisely placed a cemetery where their ashes and their glory shall sleep till time shall be no more. And where our kings have been crowned, their ancestors lay interred, and they must walk over their grandsire's head to take his crown. There is an acre sown with royal seed, the copy of the greatest change, from rich to naked, from ceiled roofs to arched coffins, from living like gods to die like men. There is enough to cool the flames of lust, to abate the heights of pride, to appease the itch of covetous desires, to sully and dash out the dissembling colours of a lustful, artificial, and imaginary beauty. There the warlike and the peaceful, the fortunate and the miserable, the beloved and the despised princes mingle their dust, and pay down their symbol of mortality, and tell all the world that when we die our ashes shall be equal to kings, and our accounts easier, and our pains or our crowns shall be less. To my apprehension it is a sad record which is left by Athenaeus concerning Ninus, the great Assyrian monarch, whose life and death is summed up in these words: "Ninus the Assyrian had an ocean of gold, and other riches more than the sand in the Caspian sea; he never saw the stars, and perhaps he never desired it; he never stirred up the holy fire among the Magi, nor touched his god with the sacred rod according to the laws; he never offered sacrifice nor worshipped the deity, nor administered justice nor spake to his people nor numbered them; but he was most valiant to eat and drink, and having mingled his wines he threw the rest upon the stones. This man is dead: behold his sepulchre. And now hear where Ninus is: 'Sometimes [once] I was Ninus, and drew the breath of a living man; but now am nothing but clay. I have nothing but what I did eat and what I served to myself in lust; that was and is all my portion. The wealth with which I was esteemed blessed, my enemies meeting together shall bear away, as the mad Thyades carry a raw goat. I am gone to hell; and when I went thither I neither carried gold, nor horse, nor silver chariot. I that wore a mitre, am now a little heap of dust.' " *H.D. (ch. i); III, 272 f.*

PRAYER

Holy and eternal Jesus, . . . take from me all vanity of spirit, lightness of fancy . . . and fantastic deceptions: let my thoughts be as my religion, plain, honest, pious, simple, prudent, and charitable. . . . Let me be wholly inebriated with love. *G.E. (Pt. i, § v); II, 144.*

The soul of a Christian is the house of God . . . but the house of God is the house of prayer. And therefore prayer is the work of the soul, whose organs are intended for instruments of the divine praises. And when every stop and pause of those instruments is but the conclusion of a collect and every breathing is a prayer, then the body becomes a temple, and the soul is the sanctuary and more private recess and place of intercourse. . . . Prayer is the "ascent of the mind to God." *G.E. (Pt. ii, § xii); II, 464.*

He that is cold and tame in his prayers hath not tasted of the deliciousness of religion and the goodness of God; he is a stranger to the secrets of the kingdom, and therefore he does not know what it is either to have hunger or satiety. . . . Fall upon your knees and grow there, and let not your desires cool nor your zeal remit, but renew it again and again. *S.W. (v); IV, 64, 66.*

There is no greater argument in the world of our spiritual danger and unwillingness to religion, than the backwardness which most men have always, and all men have sometimes, to say their prayers: so weary of their length, so glad when they are done, so witty to excuse and frustrate an opportunity. *H.L. (ch. iv); III, 175.*

Not only the interior beauties and brighter excellencies are as unfelt as ideas and abstractions are, but also the practice and common knowledge of the duty itself [prayer] are strangers to us, like the retirements of the deep, or the undiscovered treasures of the Indian hills. And this is a very great cause of the dryness and expiration of men's devotion, because our souls are so little refreshed with the waters and holy dews of meditation. We go to our prayers by chance, or order, or by determination of accidental occurrences; and we recite them as we read a book; and sometimes we are sensible of the duty, and a flash of lightning makes the room bright, and our prayers end, and the lightning is gone, and we as dark as ever: we draw our water from standing pools, which never are filled but with sudden showers, and therefore we are dry so often. *G.E. (Pt. i, § v); II, 129 f.*

If we loved passionately what we ask for daily, we should ask with hearty desires, and an earnest appetite and a present spirit; and however it be very easy to have our thoughts wander, yet it is our indifferency and lukewarmness that makes it so natural: and you may observe it, that so long as the light shines bright and the fires of devotion and desires flame out, so long the mind of a man stands close to the altar and waits upon the sacrifice; but as the fires die and desires decay, so the mind steals away and walks abroad to see the little images of beauty and pleasure which it beholds in the falling stars and little glow-worms of the world. The river that runs slow and creeps by the banks and begs leave of every turf to let it pass, is drawn into little hollownesses and spends itself in smaller portions and dies with diversion; but when it runs with vigorousness and a full stream and breaks down every obstacle, making it even as its own brow, it stays not to be tempted by little avocations and to creep into holes, but runs into the sea through full and useful channels: so is a man's prayer. *S.W. (xiii); IV, 161.*

Our prayers must be fervent, intense, earnest, and importunate, when we pray for things of high concernment and necessity. . . . According as our desires are, so are our prayers; and as our prayers are, so shall be the grace, and as that is, so shall be the measure of glory. But this admits of degrees according to the perfection or imperfection of our state of life; but it hath no other measures, but ought to be as great as it can; the bigger, the better. *H.L. (ch. iv); III, 178.*

It is a mysterious elegancy that is in the Hebrew of the Old Testament; when the Spirit of God would call any thing very great or very excellent, He calls it "of the Lord"; so "the affrightment of the Lord," that is, a great affrightment . . . and when David took the spear and water-pot from [beside] the head of Saul while he and his guards were sleeping, it is said that "the sleep of the Lord," that is, a very great sleep, was fallen upon them. Thus we read of the "flames of God" and a "land of the darkness of God," that is, vehement flames and a land of exceeding darkness: and the reason is, because when God strikes, He strikes vehemently. . . . On the other side, when He blesses He blesses excellently. . . . In proportion to all this, whatsoever is offered to God should be of the best: it should be a devout prayer, a fervent, humble, passionate supplication. He that prays otherwise must expect the curses and contempt of lukewarmness. . . . Fire will easily combine with fire, and flame marries flame; but a cold devotion and the fire of this altar can never be friendly and unite in one pyramid to ascend together to the regions of God and the element of love.

Wor. Com. (ch. ii); VIII, 75 f.

Our prayers must be the work of our hearts, not of our lips; that is, that we heartily desire what we so carefully pray for: and God knows this is not very ordinary. . . . We pray sometimes that God may be first and last in all our thoughts and yet we conceive it no great matter whether He be or no. . . . We prayer against covetousness and pride and glutony. . . . We do covetous actions and speak proud words, and have high thoughts, and do not passionately desire to have affections contrary to them, but only to such notions of the sin as we have entertained . . . and whatever our prayers are, yet it is certain our desires are so little and so content with any thing of this nature, that for very many spiritual petitions we are indifferent whether they be granted or not. . . .

When therefore you are to give sentence concerning your prayers, your prayer-book is the least thing that is to be examined; your desires are the principal, for they are the fountains both of action and passion. Desire what you pray for, for certain it is you will pray passionately if you desire fervently; prayers are but the body of the bird, desires are its angel's wings. *Wor. Com. (ch. ii); VIII, 73 ff.*

It is permitted to every man to speak his prayers, or only to think them, which is a speaking to God. Vocal or mental prayer is all one to God, but in order to us they have their several advantages. . . . Words are the arrest of the desires, and keep the spirit fixed, and in less permissions to wander from fancy to fancy. And mental prayer is apt to make the greater fervour, if it wander not; our office is more determined by words, but we then actually think of God when our spirits only speak. Mental prayer, when our spirits wander, is like a watch standing still because the spring is down; wind it up again, and it goes on regularly: but in vocal prayer, if the words run on, and the spirit wanders, the clock strikes false, the hand points not to the right hour, because something is in disorder, and the striking is nothing but noise. In mental prayer, we confess God's omniscience; in vocal prayer we call the angels to witness. *G.E. (Pt. ii, § xii); II, 482 f.*

[Consider] Moses' prayer when he spake nothing, and Hannah's, and our blessed Saviour's when He called upon His Father "with strong cries," in that great desertion of spirit when He prayed in the garden. In these prayers the spirit was bound up with the strictness and violence of intention, but could not ease itself with a flood of language and various expression. A great devotion is like a great grief, not so expressive as a moderate passion; tears spend the grief, and variety of language breathes out the devotion. *S.F.L.; V, 281.*

The first [essential] is actual or habitual attention to our prayers, which we are to procure with moral and severe endeavours, that we desire not God to hear us when we do not hear ourselves. To which purpose we must avoid, as much as our duty will permit us, multiplicity of cares and exterior employments: for a river cut into many rivulets divides also its strength, and grows contemptible, and apt to be forded by a lamb, and drunk up by a summer sun: so is the spirit of man busied in variety, and divided in itself: it abates its fervour, cools into indifferency, and becomes trifling by its dispersion and inadvertency. Aquinas was once asked, with what compendium a man might best become learned? he answered, By reading of one book: meaning, that an understanding entertained with several objects is intent upon neither, and profits not. *G.E. (Pt. ii, § xii); II, 475.*

He that means to meditate in the best order to the productions of piety, must not be inquisitive for the highest mysteries; but the plainest propositions are to him of the greatest use and evidence. For meditation is the duty of all; and therefore God hath fitted such matter for it which is proportioned to every understanding; and the greatest mysteries of Christianity are plainest, and yet most fruitful of meditation, and most useful to the production of piety. High speculations are as barren as the tops of cedars; but the fundamentals of Christianity are fruitful as the valleys or the creeping vine. For know, that it is no meditation, but it may be an illusion, when you consider mysteries to become more learned, without thoughts of improving piety. . . . It was a saying of Aegidius, "that an old and a simple woman, if she loves Jesus, may be greater than was brother Bonaventure." Want of learning, and disability to consider great secrets of theology, do not at all retard our progress to spiritual perfections. *G.E. (Pt. i, § v); II, 134.*

If you are as just in your buying and selling as you are when you are saying your prayers; if you are as chaste in your conversation as you are in your religious retirement; if your temperance be the same every day as it is in your thoughts upon a fasting day; if you wear the same habits of virtue every day in the week as you put on upon a communion day, you have more reason to think yourselves prepared, than by all the *ex tempore* piety and solemn religion that rises at the sound of a bell, and keeps her time by the calendar of the church more than by the laws of God. . . . You shall better know the state of your soul by examining how you converse with your merchant than by considering how cautiously you converse with your priest.

Wor. Com. (Ch. ii, § iii); VIII, 69.

Prayer is the peace of our spirit, the stillness of our thoughts, the evenness of recollection, the seat of meditation, the rest of our cares, and the calm of our tempest. Prayer is the issue of a quiet mind, of untroubled thoughts; it is the daughter of charity and the sister of meekness; and he that prays to God with an angry, that is, with a troubled and discomposed spirit, is like him that retires into a battle to meditate, and sets up his closet in the out-quarters of an army, and chooses a frontier garrison to be wise in.

Anger is a perfect alienation of the mind from prayer, and therefore is contrary to that attention which presents our prayers in a right line to God. For so have I seen a lark rising from his bed of grass, and soaring upwards, singing as he rises, and hopes to get to heaven and climb above the clouds; but the poor bird was beaten back with the loud sighings of an eastern wind and his motion made irregular and unconstant, descending more at every breath of the tempest than it could recover by the libration [balancing] and frequent weighing of its wings; till the little creature was forced to sit down and pant and stay till the storm was over, and then it made a prosperous flight and did rise and sing as if it had learned music and motion from an angel as he passed sometimes through the air about his ministeries here below: so is the prayer of a good man. *S.W. (v); IV, 61 f.*

A long prayer and a short differ not in their capacities of being accepted, for both of them take their value according to the fervency of spirit, and the charity of the prayer. *H.L. (ch. iv); III, 179.*

[Charity] is one of the wings of prayer, by which it flies to the throne of grace. *H.L. (ch. iv); III, 195.*

[Prayer] can put a holy restraint upon God, and detain an angel till he leave a blessing; it can open the treasures of rain and soften the iron ribs of rocks till they melt into tears and a flowing river; prayer can unclasp the girdles of the north, saying to a mountain of ice, "Be thou removed hence and cast into the bottom of the sea"; it can arrest the sun in the midst of his course and send the swift-winged winds upon our errand. And all those strange things and secret decrees and unrevealed transactions which are above the clouds and far beyond the regions of the stars, shall combine in ministry and advantages for the praying man: it cannot be but we should feel less evil, and much more good than we do, if our prayers were right. But the state of things is thus: it is an easy duty, and there are many promises, and we do it often, and yet we prevail but little. . . . Let us rectify our prayers and try what the event will be; it is worth so much at least.

Wor. Com. (ch. ii); VIII, 72 f.

Read scriptures, and then pray to God for understanding.

H.L. (ch. iv); III, 180.

All prayer must be made with faith and hope; that is, we must certainly believe we shall receive the grace which God hath commanded us to ask; and we must hope for such things which He hath permitted us to ask. And our hope shall not be vain, though we miss what is not absolutely promised, because we shall at least have an equal blessing in the denial as in the grant. *H.L. (ch. iv); III, 178.*

Whatever we beg of God, let us also work for it, if the thing be matter of duty or a consequent to industry, for God loves to bless labour. *H.L. (ch. iv); III, 180.*

If God sees the spirit broken all in pieces, and that it needs a little of the oil of gladness for its support and restitution to the capacity of its duty, He will give it. *G.E. (Pt. i, § v); II, 137.*

All thanks and praise without a right-ordered conversation, are but the echo of religion, a voice and no substance; but if those praises be sung by a heart righteous and obedient, that is singing with the spirit and singing with understanding, that is the music God delights in. *G.E. (Pt. i, § v); II, 138.*

Holy Jesus, give me the gift and spirit of prayer. *G.E. (Pt. iii, § xv); II, 668.*

Lord, let me be as constant in the ways of religion as the sun in his course, as ready to follow the intimations of Thy Spirit as little birds are to obey the directions of Thy providence and the conduct of Thy hand . . . that I may live according to the rules of nature in such things which she teaches, modestly, temperately, and affectionately, in all the parts of my natural and political relations; and that I, proceeding from nature to grace, may henceforth go on from grace to glory, the crown of all obedience, prudent and holy walking, through Jesus Christ our Lord. Amen. *G.E. (Pt. i, § iii); II, 81.*

O holy Jesu, Son of the eternal God, Thy glory is far above all heavens, and yet Thou didst descend to earth, that Thy descent might be the more gracious by how much Thy glories were admirable, and natural, and inseparable: I adore Thy holy humanity with humble veneration . . . because Thou hast personally united human nature to the eternal Word. . . . This great and glorious mystery is the honour and glory of man. It was the expectation of our fathers, who saw the mysteriousness of Thy incarnation at great and obscure distances. *G.E. (Pt. i, § ii); II, 62.*

Blessed and most holy Jesus, fountain of grace and comfort, treasure of wisdom and spiritual emanations . . . if Thou art pleased upon a design of charity or trial to cover my eyes that I may not behold the bright rays of Thy favour nor be refreshed with spiritual comforts, let Thy love support my spirit by ways insensible, and in all my needs give me such a portion as may be instrumental and incentive to performance of my duty; and in all accidents let me continue to seek Thee by prayers and humiliation and frequent desires, and the strictness of a holy life. *G.E. (Pt. i, § vii); II, 162.*

From *A prayer to be used in behalf of fools or changelings* [simpletons].

O eternal and most blessed Saviour Jesus . . . have pity upon the miserable people to whom Thou hast given life and no understanding. . . . Impute not to them their follies that are unavoidable, nor the sins which they discern not, nor the evils which they cannot understand. . . . [Let] Thy intercession prevail for them: that since they cannot glorify Thee by a free obedience, Thou mayst be glorified by Thy free mercies to them. *Collection of Offices; VIII, 672.*

From *A prayer for madmen.*

Almighty God, whose wisdom is infinite, whose mercy is eternal, whose tranquility is essential, and whose goodness hath no shore; in judgment remember mercy, and do Thou delight to magnify Thy mercy upon them who need it, but cannot ask it; who are in misery, but feel it not; who do actions without choice, or choose without discretion and sober understanding. Pity the evil they suffer, and pardon the evils that they have done, and impute not unto them the evils which they rather bear than act. . . . Lord, restore them to their health and understanding, take from them all violent passions, and remove all evil objects far from their eyes and ears; . . . suffer them not to do violence to any man, and let no man do violence to them. Let them be safe under the conduct of Thy providence and the public laws, and be innocent under the conduct of Thy holy spirit. *Collection of Offices; VIII, 672 f.*

O holy and most glorious God . . . be pleased to let Thy holy Spirit lead me in the straight paths of sanctity. . . . Throughly [thoroughly] purge the floor and granary of my heart with Thy fan, with the breath of Thy diviner Spirit, that it may be a holy repository of graces and full of benediction and sanctity. *G.E. (Pt. i, § viii); II, 170 f.*

I am nothing, I have nothing, I desire nothing but Jesus, and to be in Jerusalem, the holy city from above. Make haste, O Lord. Behold, my heart is ready, my heart is ready: come Lord Jesus, come quickly.
Wor. Com. (ch. vii, § ii); VIII, 232.

[Prayer] cures diseases without physic and makes physic to do the work of nature, and nature to do the work of grace, and grace to do the work of God, and it does miracles of accident and event. And yet prayer that does all this is of itself nothing but an ascent of the mind to God, a desiring things fit to be desired, and an expression of this desire to God. *H.L. (ch. iv); III, 176.*

Pray often, and you shall pray oftener. *H.L. (ch. iv); III, 185.*

STEPS IN MYSTICAL THEOLOGY: THE UNITIVE WAY

The first beginners in religion are employed in the mastering of their first appetites, casting out their devils, exterminating all evil customs, lessening the proclivity of habits, and countermanding the too great forwardness of vicious inclinations; and this, which divines call the purgative way, is wholly spent in actions of repentance, mortification, and self-denial. . . .

After our first step is taken, and the punitive part of repentance is resolved on, and begun, and put forward into good degrees of progress, we then enter into the illuminative way of religion. . . . If a pious soul passes to affections of greater sublimity, and intimate and more immediate, abstracted and immaterial love, it is well; only remember that the love God requires of us, is an operative, material, and communicative love, "If ye love Me, keep My commandments": so that still a good life is the effect of the sublimest meditation. . . .

Beyond this I have described, there is a degree of meditation so exalted, that it changes the very name, and is called contemplation; and it is in the unitive way of religion, that is, it consists in unions and adherences to God; it is a prayer of quietness and silence, and a meditation extraordinary, a discourse without variety, a vision and intuition of divine excellencies, an immediate entry into an orb of light, and a resolution of all our faculties into sweetnesses, affections, and starings upon the divine beauty; and is carried on to ecstasies, raptures, suspensions, elevations, abstractions, and apprehensions beatifical. . . .

But this is a thing not to be discoursed of, but felt: and although in other sciences the terms must first be known, and then the rules and conclusions scientifical; here it is otherwise: for first, the whole experience of this must be obtained before we can so much as know what it is; and the end must be acquired first, the conclusion before the premises. They that pretend to these heights call them the secrets of the kingdom; but they are such which no man can describe; such which God hath not revealed in the publication of the gospel; such for the acquiring of which there are no means prescribed. *G.E.* (*Pt. i,* § *v*)*; II, 136-40.*

From [meditation] the man rises to devotion, and mental prayer, and intercourse with God; and after that, he rests in the bosom of beatitude and is swallowed up with the comprehensions of love and contemplation. *G.E.* (*Pt. i,* § *v*)*; II, 135.*

For him that considers God's mercies and dwells awhile in that depth, it is hard not to talk wildly and without art and order of discoursings. St. Peter talked he knew not what, when he entered into a cloud with Jesus upon Mount Tabor, though it passed over him like the little curtains that ride upon the north wind and pass between the sun and us. And when we converse with a light greater than the sun, and taste a sweetness more delicious than the dew of heaven, and in our thoughts entertain the ravishments and harmony of that atonement which reconciles God to man and man to felicity, it will be more easily pardoned if we should be like persons that admire much and say but little; and indeed we can best confess the glories of the Lord by dazzled eyes and a stammering tongue, and a heart overcharged with the miracles of this infinity. *S.S.* (*xxv*)*; IV, 634.*

I shall not need to urge the mysteriousness of some points in scripture which *ex natura rei* are hard to be understood though very plainly represented. For there are some *secreta theologiae* which are only to be understood by persons very holy and spiritual; which are rather to be felt than discoursed of. And therefore if peradventure they be offered to public consideration they will therefore be opposed because they run the same fortune with many other questions: that is, not to be understood, and so much the rather because their understanding . . . [is] not the results of logic and philosophy, nor yet of public revelation, but of the public spirit privately working. *L.P.; V, 419.*

Perfect persons should serve God out of mere love of God and the divine excellencies, without the considerations of either heaven or hell. Such a thing as that is talked of in mystical theology, and I doubt not but many good persons come to that growth of charity that the goodness and excellency of God are more incumbent and actually pressing upon their spirit than any considerations of reward. But then I shall add this, that when persons come to that height of grace, or contemplation rather, and they love God for Himself, and do their duties in order to the fruition of Him and His pleasure—all that is but heaven in another sense and under another name, just as the mystical theology is the highest duty and the choicest part of obedience under a new method.

S.S. (*xv*)*; IV, 511.*

In many things she [Reason] knows nothing but the face of the article: the mysteries of faith are oftentimes like cherubim's heads placed over the propitiatory, where you may see a clear and a bright face and golden wings, but there is no body to be handled; there is light and splendour upon the brow, but you may not grasp it; and though you see the revelation clear and the article plain, yet the reason of it we cannot see at all; that is, the whole knowledge which we can have here is dark and obscure. . . . We can see what, but not why, and what we do see is the least part of that which does not appear; but in these cases our understanding is to submit, and wholly to be obedient, but not to enquire further. *Ductor (Bk. i, ch. ii); IX, 64.*

The secrets of the kingdom of heaven are not understood truly and thoroughly but by the sons of the kingdom; and by them too in several degrees and to various purposes: but to evil persons the whole system of this wisdom is insipid and flat, dull as the foot of a rock, and unlearned as the elements of our mother tongue; but so are mathematics to a Scythian boor, and music to a camel. *G.E. (pref.); II, 36.*

He that desires to enter furthest into the secrets of this mystery [the Eucharist] and to understand more than others, can better learn by love than by enquiry. . . . If he will . . . pass through the mystery with great devotion and purest simplicity, and converse with the purities of the sacrament frequently and with holy intention, this man shall understand more by his experience than the greatest clerks can by all their subtilties, the commentaries of the doctors, and the glosses of inquisitive men. "The love of the Lord," saith the wise man,* "passeth all things for illumination." *Wor. Com. (ch. i); VIII, 47.*

Although the scriptures themselves are written by the Spirit of God, yet they are written within and without: and besides the light that shines upon the face of them, unless there be a light shining within our hearts, unfolding the leaves and interpreting the mysterious sense of the Spirit, convincing our consciences and preaching to our hearts, to look for Christ in the leaves of the gospel is to look for the living amongst the dead. There is a life in them, but . . . unless the Spirit of God be the *promo-condus,* we shall never draw it forth. *Un. D.; VIII, 379 f.*

Many illusions have come in the likeness of visions, and absurd fancies under the pretence of raptures; and what some have called the spirit of prophecy, hath been the spirit of lying: and contemplation hath been nothing but melancholy and unnatural lengths; and stillness of prayer hath been a mere dream and hypochrondriacal devotion and hath ended in pride or despair. . . .

It was . . . an excellent desire of St. Bernard, who was as likely as

*** Jesus, the Son of Sirach: Ecclesiasticus XXV, 11.**

any to have . . . altitudes of speculation: . . . "I pray God grant to me peace of spirit, joy in the holy Ghost, to compassionate others in the midst of my mirth, to be charitable in simplicity, to rejoice with them that rejoice, and to mourn with them that mourn; and with these I shall be content. Other exaltations of devotion I leave to apostles and apostolic men; the high hills are for the harts and the climbing goats, the stony rocks and the recesses of the earth for the conies." It is more healthful and nutritive to dig the earth and to eat of her fruits than to stare upon the greatest glories of the heavens and live upon the beams of the sun. . . .

Familiarity with God, which is an affection of friendship . . . is part of every man's inheritance that is a friend of God. But when familiarity with God shall be esteemed a privilege of singular and eminent persons, not communicated to all the faithful . . . it is an effect of pride and a mistake in judgment concerning the very same thing which the old divines call the unitive way. *G.E. (Pt. i, § v); II, 141 ff.*

Let [meditations] be as exalted as the capacity of the person and subject will endure, up to the height of contemplation; but if contemplation comes to be a distinct thing and something besides or beyond a distinct degree of virtuous meditation, it is lost to all sense and religion and prudence: let no man be hasty to eat of the fruits of paradise before his time. *G.E. (Pt. i, § v); II, 143.*

These disciples asked of Christ where He dwelt: Jesus answered, "Come and see." It was an answer very expressive of our duty in this instance. It is not enough for us to understand where Christ inhabits or where He is to be found, for our understandings may follow Him afar off and we receive no satisfaction unless it be to curiosity. . . . The secrets of spiritual benediction are understood only by them to whom they are conveyed, even by the children of His house: "come and see."
G.E. (Pt. ii, § x); II, 289 f.

The seed of God is the Spirit, which hath a plastic power to efform us "into the image of the sons of God"; and as long as this remains in us, while the Spirit dwells in us, we cannot sin; that is, it is against our natures, our reformed natures, to sin. *S.S. (i); IV, 339.*

By the spirit of a new life we are made new creatures, capable of a new state, entitled to another manner of duration, enabled to do new and greater actions in order to higher ends. We have new affections, new understandings, new wills; "all things are become new."
S.S. (ii); IV, 347 f.

There is in every righteous man a new vital principle; the Spirit of grace is the Spirit of wisdom, and teaches us by secret inspirations, by proper arguments, by actual persuasions, by personal applications, by effects and energies; and as the soul of a man is the cause of all his vital operations, so is the Spirit of God the life of that life, and the cause of all actions and productions spiritual. . . .

[God] opens the heart, and creates a new one; and without this new creation, this new principle of life, we may hear the word of God, but we can never understand it; we hear the sound, but are never the better; unless there be in our hearts a secret conviction by the Spirit of God, the gospel in itself is a dead letter, and worketh not in us the light and righteousness of God. . . .

[The man who understands as a son of God . . . by love] does not only understand the sermons of the Spirit, and perceives their meaning, but he pierces deeper and knows the meaning of that meaning; that is, the secret of the Spirit, . . . that which gives . . . activity to the soul. And the reason is, because he hath a divine principle within him, and a new understanding; that is, plainly, he hath love, and that's more than knowledge. . . . No scriptures can build you up a holy building to God, unless the love of God be in your hearts. *Un. D.; VIII, 375 ff.*

There is in the things of God to them which practice them a deliciousness that makes us love them, and that love admits us into God's cabinet, and strangely clarifies the understanding by the purification of the heart. For when our reason is raised up by the Spirit of Christ, it is turned quickly into experience; when our faith relies upon the principles of Christ, it is changed into vision. And so long as we know God only in the ways of man, by contentious learning, by arguing and dispute, we see nothing but the shadow of Him, and in that shadow we meet with many dark appearances, little certainty, and much conjecture. But when we know Him with the eyes of holiness, and the intuition of gracious experiences, with a quiet spirit and the peace of enjoyment, then we shall hear what we never heard, and see what our eyes never saw; then the mysteries of godliness shall be opened unto us, and clear as the windows of the morning.

There is a sort of God's dear servants who walk in perfectness; . . . and they have a degree of clarity and divine knowledge more than we can discourse of, and more certain than the demonstrations of geometry, brighter than the sun, and indeficient as the light of heaven. . . .

But I shall say no more of this at this time, for this is to be felt and not to be talked of; and they that never touched it with their finger, may secretly perhaps laugh at it in their heart, and be never the wiser. All that I shall now say of it is, that a good man is united unto God as a flame touches a flame, and combines into splendour and to glory. . . . These are the friends of God, and they best know God's mind and they only that are so, know how much such men do know. They have a special "unction from above": so that now you are come to the top of all; this is the highest round of the ladder, and the angels stand upon it: they dwell in love and contemplation. *Un. D.; VIII, 379 f.*

"God's secrets are to Himself and the sons of His house," saith the Jewish proverb. Love is the great instrument of divine knowledge, that is "the height of all that is to be taught or learned." Love is obedience, and we learn His words best when we practise them. . . .

He that hath passed from his childhood in grace . . . and from thence is become an old disciple, and strong and grown old in religion and the conversation of the Spirit: this man best understands the secret and undiscernible economy; he feels this unintelligible mystery, and sees with his heart what his tongue can never express and his metaphysics can never prove. *Un. D.; VIII, 386 f.*

Notes to the Introductory Essay

1. Letter to John Kenyon (Nov. 3, 1814), *Letters of Samuel Taylor Coleridge,* edited by Hartley Coleridge, II, 640.
2. *The Golden Grove, Selected Passages from the Sermons and Writings of Jeremy Taylor,* edited with introduction by Logan Pearsall Smith, Clarendon Press, 1930, p. xxvii.
3. *Ibid.* Quotations in the following paragraph are taken from pp. xxix-lxii.
4. Edmund Gosse, *Jeremy Taylor,* Macmillan, 1904, p. 47.
5. Reginald Heber, *Life of Jeremy Taylor,* prefacing the edition of Taylor's works, 1859, I, ccxlii.
6. Coleridge, *op. cit.,* p. 640 f.
7. Heber, *op. cit.,* I, lxxxvii.
8. Jane E. Harrison, *Prolegomena to the Study of Greek Religion,* Cambridge Un. Press, 1903, p. 156.
9. Paolo Sarpi Veneto [Pietro Soave Polano], *The Historie of the Councel of Trent,* translated into English by Nathanael Brent, London, 1620, p. 248.
10. William Chillingworth, *The Religion of Protestants,* tenth edition, 1742, ch. IV, § 17, p. 204.
11. Edith Hamilton, *The Greek Way to Western Civilization,* Mentor Books, 1948, p. 143.
12. Aeschylus, *Agamemnon,* translated by Herbert Weir Smith, Loeb Classical Library, lines 175-80.
13. For treatment in addition to Heber's see Marjorie Hope Nicolson, *Philological Quarterly,* VIII, 329; Hugh Ross Williamson, *Jeremy Taylor,* pp. 153-58; C. J. Stranks, *The Life and Writings of Jeremy Taylor,* 251 ff.
14. Gosse, *op. cit.,* p. 154.
15. For a detailed treatment of the *Ductor,* see Thomas Wood, as cited in appended bibliography.
16. For a detailed account of Taylor's harried relations to the Presbyterian ministers, see C. J. Stranks, *op. cit.,* chapter X; Hugh Ross Williamson, *op. cit.,* pp. 159-63.

Brief Bibliography for the Study of Taylor and Seventeenth-Century Religious Thought in England

The standard edition of Taylor is *The Whole Works of the Right Rev. Jeremy Taylor, D.D.,* edited with notes and an introductory biography by Reginald Heber, and revised by Charles Page Eden and [for the *Ductor Dubitantium*] Alexander Taylor.

Antoine, Sister Mary Salome. *Rhetoric of Jeremy Taylor's Prose,* 1946.

Brinkley, R. F. *English Poetry of the XVIIth Century, with introduction.*

Brown, W. J. *Jeremy Taylor,* 1925 [a treatment of Taylor's theology].

Burnet, Bishop Gilbert. *An Exposition of the Thirty-nine Articles; History of His Own Time; History of the Reformation in England.*

Butler, Dom Cuthbert. *Western Mysticism.*

Cambridge Bibliography of English Literature. Cambridge History of English Literature.

Coleridge, S. T. *Notes on English Divines.*

Evelyn, John. *Diaries; Correspondence.*

Faber, Albertus Otto. *A Remonstrance in Reference to the Act to Prevent and Suppress Seditious Conventicles.*

Forster, John. *Sir John Eliot, a Biography.*

Fuller, Thomas. *Church History of Britain,* edited by John S. Brewer, Vols. 5 and 6.

George, E. A. *Seventeenth Century Men of Latitude.*

Glicksman, H. "Figurative Quality in Jeremy Taylor's *Holy Dying,*" *Sewanee Review,* October 1922.

Gosse, Sir Edmund. *Jeremy Taylor.*

Hallam, Henry. *Constitutional History of England; Literature of Europe.*

Heber, Bishop Reginald. *Life of Jeremy Taylor,* in the *Whole Works,* Vol. I.

Heylyn, Peter. *Ecclesia Restaurata, or The History of the Reformation of the Church of England.*

Holy Dying, Rule and Exercises of. Edited and with an introduction by Thomas S. Kepler, 1952.

Hutchinson, F. E. *George Herbert,* with introduction.

Jones, Rufus. *Spiritual Reformers in the 16th and 17th Centuries; Studies in Mystical Religion; The Church's Debt to Heretics.*

Lecky, W. E. H. *History of the Rise and Influence of the Spirit of Rationalism in Europe.*

MacKinnon, Flora Isabel. *The Philosophical Writings of Henry More,* with introduction and bibliography.

Mosheim, J. L. von. *Institutes of Ecclesiastical History.*

Nicolson, Marjorie H. "New Material on Jeremy Taylor," *Philological Quarterly,* October, 1929, VIII, 321-34.

Powicke, Frank J. "Jeremy Taylor and his Doctrine of Toleration," *Constructive Quarterly,* September, 1915.

Rollins, George A. "Contribution of Jeremy Taylor to Modern Preaching," *Methodist Review,* March, 1924.

Rust, Bishop George. "A Funeral Sermon Preached at the Obsequies of the Right Reverend Father in God, Jeremy, Lord Bishop of Down," included in *The Whole Works* of Taylor, Vol. I, p. cccii.

Saintsbury, George. *A History of English Prosody from the Twelfth Century to the Present Day,* Vol. 2; *Minor Poets of the Caroline Period,* with introduction.

Simpkinson, C. H. *Life and Times of William Laud.*

Smith, Logan Pearsall. *The Golden Grove, Selections from the Sermons and Writings of Jeremy Taylor,* with introduction by Smith and bibliography of Taylor's writings by R. G. Hardy.

Sorley, W. R. *A History of English Philosophy,* with detailed bibliography.

Stranks, C. J. *The Life and Writings of Jeremy Taylor,* 1952 [valuable new material and bibliography].

Tulloch, John. *Rational Theology and Christian Philosophy in England in the 17th Century.*

Turnor, Edmund. *Characters of Eminent Men in the Reigns of Charles I and II,* taken from the works of Lord Chancellor Clarendon.

Underhill, Evelyn. *Mysticism.*

Walker, John. *An Attempt towards Recovering an Account of the Numbers and Sufferings of the Clergy of the Church of England.*

Williamson, Hugh Ross. *Jeremy Taylor,* 1952.

Wood, Thomas. *English Casuistical Divinity during the Seventeenth Century, with Special Reference to Jeremy Taylor,* 1952.

Worley, George. *Jeremy Taylor, a sketch of his life and times with a popular exposition of his works,* 1904.

Designed by Guenther K. Wehrhan

Printed and Serviced by Kutztown Publishing Co., Kutztown

Binding by Arnold Bindery, Reading